DISCOVERING CHILD POVERTY

The creation of a policy agenda from 1800 to the present

Lucinda Platt

First published in Great Britain in January 2005 by

The Policy Press
University of Bristol
Fourth Floor
Beacon House
Queen's Road
Bristol BS8 1QU
UK

Tel +44 (0)117 331 4054
Fax +44 (0)117 331 4093
e-mail tpp-info@bristol.ac.uk
www.policypress.org.uk

British Library Cataloguing in Publication Data
A catalogue record for this book is available from the British Library.

Library of Congress Cataloging-in-Publication Data
A catalog record for this book has been requested.

ISBN 1 86134 583 6 paperback

Lucinda Platt is a Lecturer in the Department of Sociology, University of
Essex, UK.

Cover design by Qube Design Associates, Bristol.
Front cover: photograph supplied by kind permission of Philip Wolmuth/
Panos Pictures.
Printed and bound in Great Britain by Latimer Trend, Plymouth.

Dedication
In memory of Norman Platt, 1920-2004

Contents

Acknowledgements

I am grateful to Justine Coulson of Save the Children/Young Lives, who originally set me thinking along the lines of this book. I would like to thank the Department of Sociology at the University of Essex for allowing me study leave, and the Institute of Social and Economic Research, also at the University of Essex, for granting me a Visiting Fellowship during which I worked on the project. I am grateful to the readers of both the proposal and of the draft of the book for their helpful and constructive comments. I am also grateful for the close reading and detailed (and encouraging!) comments of David Colclough. The resulting book has undoubtedly benefited substantially from these responses. I, however, bear full responsibility for what follows and for any remaining errors. Dawn Rushen and all at The Policy Press have been a pleasure to work with; and I would like to thank them for all they have done to see this through to publication. My thanks also to the Joseph Rowntree Charitable Trust for permission to reproduce material from the works of B.S. Rowntree. This book is dedicated to the memory of my father, Norman Platt, who died in January of this year. Profoundly missed, he yet remains a constant inspiration to me in all I do.

ONE

Introduction: scope and argument of the book

Over the last two hundred years, Britain has witnessed a dramatic shift in the level of concern and attention paid to the issue of child poverty. Child poverty is now high on the policy agenda and is broadly recognised as a problem for society and a fit subject for policy intervention. By setting the development of this policy agenda in historical perspective, this book aims to illuminate both the complex relationship between research and policy, and the way in which policy constructs its own objects of intervention. The role of research into child poverty has sometimes been perceived as being simply about identifying extent, causes and solutions, on which policy makers can then act. As this book argues, however, child poverty becomes politically salient only at certain moments and under certain conditions. Further, the emotive power of childhood, which makes a political imperative out of children's disadvantage, is also mediated to a greater or lesser extent by particular ideological and political concerns prevailing at different times. Research can, nevertheless, help to create the conditions and to set the parameters for the ways in which governments respond when they do so. The discovery of child poverty and its place at the forefront of the current political agenda have been, then, both a matter of the quantification, study and accounts of child poverty *and* the recognition of such accounts and their relevance to the polity.

This book provides a broad introduction to developments in child poverty research and the fluctuating attention paid to child poverty over an extended period. A historical understanding of child poverty and the development of child poverty research is an important element to grasping one of the most topical issues of today. As Paul Pierson points out in his discussion of the ways, and extent to which, welfare state institutions themselves influence the conditions surrounding possibilities for their change,

> Instead of turning to history for analogous processes, historically grounded analysis should be based upon a recognition that social-policy change unfolds over time. The emphasis on the impact of inherited policy structures illustrates this point. A historical perspective

highlights the fact that today's policymakers must operate in an environment fundamentally conditioned by policies inherited from the past. (Pierson, 1994, p 9)

By looking at state intervention in the lives of poor children since 1800, this account explores how their poverty rendered them a target for state controls, while those same interventions reinforced the perception of them as children by essence and poor by accident. By taking this longer view it becomes possible both to understand and to interrogate family policy, and in particular income maintenance policy, for children as it operated at the very end of the 20th century. Moreover, in taking such a broad historical sweep, it is important to pay attention to the ways that debates and interpolations into debates were constructed. This book, therefore, places a particular emphasis on quotation from some of the most influential documents or figures to demonstrate the language and expression in which research and commentary were conducted. We see from such quotations how concerns, insights and imperatives were couched and how they related to what were regarded as relevant positions. A core element of this book is, then, the inclusion of direct reference to, and quotation from, relevant works across the period, the better to understand both continuities and changes in the formulation of the problem of child poverty and responses to it.

The temporal scope of this book is in one sense arbitrary. Nevertheless, the choice of a two-hundred year trajectory does have a number of advantages. By 1800, the industrial revolution was well advanced, the urbanization of the British population was underway and the increase in population that was to cause so much anxiety was being noted. The period from 1800 can, then, be read as one in which there was a gradual growth in social policy, with a number of critical step-changes at various points, most notably in the 'welfare state' settlement marked by legislation in the areas of education, social insurance, social assistance and health between 1944-48. Other crucial moments can be seen in the 1834 Poor Law Amendment which restructured the provision of poor relief in Britain and had a legacy that extended to 1948 (and possibly beyond); while the introduction of state education in 1870 was a further watershed in the development of policy and one which created future possibilities for intervention in family life. Finally, the period from 1997 is one in which the elimination of child poverty has become an explicit target of government.

In addition, the period since 1800 can be identified as one that saw the development of a more distinct, rigidly defined and more universal notion of the child and the nature of childhood. In fact, it is part of the argument of this book that the distinct status of the child was itself partly created through the operation of social policy. In relation to poverty research, it was only in the second half of the period covered by this book that there was a clear working definition of what constituted poverty. It was only at this point that the measurement and analysis of a specific phenomenon of child poverty became possible. Nevertheless, the continuities and discontinuities in relation to the definition and quantification of poverty in the 20th century and perspectives on 'the poor' and poor relief in the 19th century are an essential part of understanding poverty research.

At the other end of the time period, in May 2000, Gordon Brown declared

> Action on child poverty is the obligation this generation owes to the next: to millions of children who should not be growing up in poverty: children who because of poverty, deprivation and the lack of opportunity have been destined to fail even before their life's journey has begun, children for whom we know – unless we act – life will never be fair. Children in deprived areas who need, deserve and must have a government on their side, a government committed to and fighting for social justice. (Brown, 2000)

In this he was following up on the commitment made by the government that children should be the top priority for the Labour administration. This had been expressed by the Prime Minister in his 1999 lecture, 'Beveridge Revisited: a welfare state for the 21st century', where he declared that

> Poverty should not be a birthright. Being poor should not be a life sentence…. Our historic aim will be for ours to be the first generation to end child poverty, and it will take a generation. It is a 20-year mission but I believe it can be done. (Blair, 1999, p 17)

There are two things noticeable about these statements: first, their acknowledgement of extensive poverty in the UK; and second, the imperative for state action which that acknowledgement brings. In fact, the prevalence of child poverty and the obligation on the government to respond to child poverty are inseparably connected. Child poverty can only be recognised as a particular social problem once childhood is acknowledged as having a sacrosanct claim to interest, regardless of parental behaviour or economic position. At the same time, the recognition of childhood as being singular and liable to protection renders children ever more directly dependant on their immediate family for increasing periods of time. This dependence in turn results in some forms of support being most appropriately delivered through the parents: while certain services, such as education, can be delivered directly to the child, income maintenance aspects of social policy reach the child via their parent(s). Yet if the child's interest is paramount through virtue of being a child, then the parent's, by definition, cannot be; and thus there is a reluctance to assist parents directly with a role that they have (voluntarily) taken on. This presents governments with the conundrum of how financially to support children without 'rewarding' the parents; and how to achieve the correct balance between parent and state in supporting children.

The centrality of child welfare by the end of the 20th century was implicit within the growth of social policy from 1800, which not only responded to children as a source of concern but also constructed them as such. As Hendrick puts it,

> ... the history of children and childhood is inescapably inseparable from the history of social policy. We cannot hope to understand the former without an appreciation of the latter. No other sector of the population has been so closely identified with the expansion and multiplication of these policies since the 1870s, and with the growth of the State and its 'expert' agencies. (Hendrick, 1994, p xii)

In 1800 there was no state schooling and education was largely a prerogative of the ruling classes; in 2004 schooling is compulsory for all children between the ages of 5 and 16 – and remaining in education up to 18 has become a normative expectation. In 1800 the only forms of child support operated locally (and variably) through parish poor relief to families. By 2004 a complex multi-tiered system of support for children is in operation with a universal child benefit as the base and the child tax credit as an income-related supplement reaching relatively far up the income scale. In 1800, child labour was unregulated and children worked according to their social position and capability. In 2004 there are systematic regulations in place which prohibit work for those aged under 13 and heavily restrict it (by hours, type and time of day) for those aged 14 and 15.

This book traces these developments and attempts to shed light on how the innovations in empirical work and the rise of the social survey contributed to changes in policy. It makes the case that the very development and utilisation of large-scale empirical research were products of the ideological, economic, social, religious and political currents that also critically fashioned social policy across the period. While research findings were pertinent to much policy change, there has not been a transparent translation from evidence to evidence-based policy. The relationship between research and policy has, instead, been mediated by the ability and willingness of policy makers to respond to particular findings, and by the forms in which those findings were presented. Thus, 'evidence' only became treated as such if it could be made to fit with existing economic and ideological conditions. The arguments from empirical work were convincing only to the extent to which they could accommodate the prevailing political context within which policy makers operated and by which they were informed.

Furthermore, this book shows that the development of policy itself has implications for research. It changes what is possible and what direction research takes. For example, the reorganisation of the Poor Law in 1834, with a much stronger emphasis on institutionalisation, rendered paupers a clearly identifiable and distinct body. They could thus be studied, and compared and contrasted to the 'respectable' poor; and ideas of socialisation versus heredity could be explored and pursued with pauper children. The introduction of compulsory schooling in 1880 enabled investigation of the child population – both their mental characteristics and their physical development – on an unprecedented scale. Claims on health insurance (which was legislated for workers in 1911) revealed the shocking condition of women employees' health, while the poor condition of non-insured women's health (including that of most mothers) was only fully revealed by the introduction of the National Health Service 37 years later. Unemployment insurance, also introduced in 1911, enabled the unemployed to be counted and hence the scale of the problem and the number of child dependants it affected to be evaluated, especially as it was extended to more and more employees in the 1920s and 1930s. The counting and investigation made possible by policy also furthered understanding of policy, and could stimulate its development.

The final, though related, issue demonstrated in this account is the extent to which policy itself constructs the subject for research. Child poverty research is impossible without a clear notion of the child and why children's poverty is a particular problem. Through education, child labour restrictions and provision for children by means of family allowances (later child benefit), the state created the space within which ideas of childhood and its unique value could develop. Such ideas, in turn, prompted further investigation and the need for additional policy response. These conceptual developments and concerns with child poverty can also been seen as continuing to form both research and policy agendas not only in the UK but also further afield.

In surveying the developments in research on child poverty and policy responses over the last two centuries and their relationship and interaction, this book highlights a number of themes, which run through and structure it. First, it emphasises the complexity of the relationship between research and policy. That is, research impacts may occur neither at the time of the research, nor in ways that are predictable. The influence of research is not necessarily in the direction in which researchers intend and is mediated by the options available to policy makers at a particular time. For child poverty research to be accorded attention it has needed to be both radical and to relate to its time and place. That is, the nature of research and its influence will vary with the political complexion of the country and with ideological and religious factors. It has both to make an impact but also to accord, at least in part, with existing mores.

Second, as well as drawing attention to the relationship between child policy and the delineation of childhood, this account makes explicit the association between children's and families' – or more particularly women's – welfare. Interventions for children often assume the interconnectedness of both the status and the concerns of women and children. This acknowledges the extent to which mothers' welfare is often bound up with that of their children (Lewis, 1980); but it can also cause child poverty policy to be obstructed, through political resistance to women's concerns.

The third theme is one also highlighted by Hendrick: the issue of children as 'investments', that is, the recognition of children in terms of their future potential and as embodiments of 'the future' (Hendrick, 2003, pp 14-16). In the early years of the 20th century child poverty was not simply an issue of current concern, but was tied up with anticipations about the future economic, military, cultural and moral state of the nation. In so far as child poverty could be shown to have negative future consequences, it provided a focus for political mobilisation. The form this political mobilisation took varied over time according to the context and contemporary anxieties, but can be seen, nevertheless, as a recurrent theme up to the present day. For example, the Chancellor, Gordon Brown, in his budget speech of 1999 (and many times thereafter), famously declared that children "are 20 per cent of the people but they are 100 per cent of the future" (Brown, 1999).

The main aims of the book are, then, to consider the increasing salience and sophistication of social research; to outline some of the principal moments and figures in poverty research over the period; and to provide an analysis of the extent to which, and the ways in which, policy responded to these findings. The book is therefore structured as follows: Chapter Two provides a brief overview of the relevant developments in research, and of the contexts in which they took place. The chapter provides an introduction to the principal figures who feature in the book and a broad chronology of research innovations and influences. In Chapter Three, I consider the question of child labour. Here the argument focuses on campaigns and legislation that were critical to subsequent developments in child welfare and to the construction of both children and women as dependants in social policy. The campaigns and legislation were little influenced by empirical research as such, but rather reveal the ability of campaigners to mobilise particular sentiments and ideas for a cause. Chapter Four treats the question of education. Education presented an alternative occupation for children in the absence of employment. It was also increasingly regarded as essential to national well-being; and yet state intervention was avoided for many years as an undesirable interference. Nevertheless, both the restriction of child labour and the introduction of state education were critical in sanctioning state interference in, and responsibility for, children's lives. Labour restriction and compulsory education, while not transparently increasing the well-being of the child, created the conditions under which child welfare research and policy could more fully develop. They did this through constituting a child population, which could be subject to observation and measurement and be accessible to intervention.

Restriction of employment and compulsory education had major implications for the well-being of the poorest families and their children. At the same time these interventions contributed to both the identification of poor children and to the recognition of them as having particular calls upon the state. Child welfare could never be fully divorced from family welfare. This resulted in ongoing tensions between research demonstrating child poverty and the consequent policy imperative to do something about it, and fears about subsidising 'irresponsible' parents. Chapter Five treats this central issue of ambivilence in recognising child poverty and responding to child poverty research, alongside discussion of the related areas of child (and maternal) health and welfare, looking at the period up to the introduction of family allowances in 1945. The period since 1945 is covered in Chapter Six, which takes up these issues surrounding the identification of child poverty and its intersection with other interventions in children's lives to explore the policy response and the relationship between child poverty and policy. In the end, policy can be seen as being increasingly informed by systematic research on child poverty. Yet policy makers have persisted in modifying the conclusions of research, sometimes dramatically, to produce a compromise between concern with child poverty and other political and economic concerns. Chapter Seven pulls the strands of the book together in a reflection on the status of child poverty on the policy agenda and the role of research within that.

Discovering child poverty demonstrates how concern with the alleviation of child poverty and its empirical investigation have developed alongside, and are implicated in, one another. We live at a time when an apparent consensus has been achieved in relation to the imperative to abolish child poverty. Yet history shows how other periods of consensus have emerged only to disintegrate. Moreover, a historical perspective illuminates the continuities in discourses around child poverty that can occur alongside major transitions in treatment; and it reveals how the apparently beneficent approach to children and their welfare is still embedded in language and ideas which emerged in more punitive contexts or were concerned with agendas, such as nation-building, that were distinct from a primary concern with the well-being of children.

TWO

The conditions for child poverty: context and chronology

This chapter outlines the development of empirical research and the social survey with its ability to define and quantify child poverty. It connects developments in research to the economic, political and religious currents of the time and to the background of the individual researchers, and outlines subsequent developments or modifications in child poverty research following the development of the prototypical social surveys. It also describes the contested nature of empirical investigation, which has not simply been the preserve of disinterested researchers; and it shows how the development of statistics was allied to debates concerning the value and quality of human life, which came into focus with studies of poverty. It goes on to look at succeeding developments and measures of child poverty, including the 'rediscovery of poverty' in the 1950s and 1960s. It charts the ongoing efforts of researchers better to render the reality of poverty both meaningful and immediate to publics and governments. It provides the context for the consideration of child poverty and policy, which constitutes the succeeding chapters.

The background to and development of empirical investigation

According to Poovey (1998), the end of the 18th century marked a shift in approaches to numbers and counting, whereby numbers became stripped of the Christian Platonic significance that had characterised that understanding hitherto. Instead they began to be regarded as without moral connotation and to hold the ability to support or challenge theoretical positions or presuppositions. For Poovey, it is Thomas Malthus who exemplifies this transition in approaches to argument and the collection of numerical data. She highlights Malthus's *An essay on the principle of population* (first published in a short version in 1798; the expanded edition, which is the one generally discussed was published in 1803) in part because it was highly influential and controversial – with its influence lasting well into the 20th century and the neo-Malthusian movement[1]. But the work also forms a highly pertinent text for consideration because the influence and controversy stemmed not simply from its underlying ideas but also from the way it advocated (and used) empirical and observational data.

Malthus was a clergyman living through a period of dramatic demographic and industrial change. The population in England saw an unprecedented expansion in the late 18th and early 19th centuries: from around 1750, increased fertility rates were sustained by younger age at marriage and improved chances of survival for infants (Coleman, 2000). Alongside a decline in the death rate, this resulted in a significant year-on-year growth of the population. The population of England and Wales expanded from around 5.5 million in 1700 to 9 million by 1801 and 18 million in 1851 (Woods, 1996). The annual population increase peaked in the 1830s with a rate of increase of around 1.3% a year (Coleman, 2000). This population increase fed (and benefited from) the processes of industrialisation, but at the same time caused concern about the sustainability of population expansion. There was at this time increased attention to understanding the workings of industrial and economic processes and the ways in which industrialisation had come into being and expanded so rapidly.

One of the most comprehensive and influential expositions of the economic processes at work was offered in 1796 by Adam Smith in *An inquiry into the nature and causes of the wealth of nations* (Smith, 1976 [1776])[2]. Smith's exposition of free market ideology argued that men operated on the basis of self-interest. He claimed that markets were the means by which people could express and act on this self-interest, and that, if allowed to operate freely, they created a balance or 'equilibrium' within economic affairs and society. He argued that state intervention in markets was detrimental to their efficiency and hence to wider prosperity. Arguments for intervention had to be set against concerns that any such interventions would distort the market and undermine individual responsibility. Smith can also be associated with the shift in political economy that stressed awareness of observed conditions and a move to greater empirical analysis. The political position known as laissez-faire associated with his ideas was a dominant force in government and policy making throughout the 19th century. Anxiety about the state creating perverse incentives, whereby individual self-interest would make people act in a way considered undesirable, continued to be a feature of social policy throughout the period. Laissez-faire was not simply a product of an influential text, however; it was also a way of explaining and understanding the major changes that were taking place in society. It was both produced by these shifts and contributed to their furtherance.

It was also related to a moral philosophical position which, in stressing individual agency, also emphasised individualism and individual responsibility, including the responsibility of parents to their children. As John Stuart Mill put it in 1859, "to bring a child into existence without a fair prospect of being able, not only to provide food for its body, but instruction and training for its mind, is a moral crime, both against the unfortunate offspring and against society" (Mill, 1991 [1859], p 115), (although he then went on to specify the conditions under which the state would be obliged to take over from the parent). The simpler, but extremely popular, work of Smiles later in the century continued to emphasise values of individual effort and responsibility in, for example, such works as *Self-help* (Smiles, 1897), first published in 1859, with multiple (and revised) editions following, and *Thrift* (Smiles, 1885). In these works, poverty is argued to be a 'happy state' if it is 'respectable' poverty, while they simultaneously imply that effort is all that is required to overcome disadvantaged origins. At the same time, the stress on individual responsibility was not the only perspective that was maintained throughout the century. The more benign (if paternalistic) attitude to distress and impoverishment that we associate with much of the popular literature of the period – literature which often (as in the works of Collins or Dickens) regarded itself as having a social role – meant that an increased role for the state could also command more support. Thus, for example, John Ruskin, writing in 1867, expressed in no uncertain terms the view that the state was effectively responsible for the well-being of its children: "I hold it for indisputable, that the first duty of a State is to see that every child born therein shall be well housed, clothed, fed and educated, till it attain years of discretion. But in order to the effecting this the Government must have an authority over the people of which we now do not so much as dream" (Ruskin, 1994 [1867] Letter xiii, p 79). And even those members of the Charity Organisation Society who strongly resisted the state undermining parental responsibility through, for example, providing free school meals, could at the same time perceive an advantage in the greater systemisation offered by coordinated (and professionalised) interventions.

The development and influence of liberal individualism, and the tension with a more interventionist and beneficent approach, is linked to major changes in the organisation and structure of society that had come about with the industrial revolution. These included urban expansion, the emergence of employment cycles, and the separation of home and employment, with the removal of much productive work from the home and a large, concentrated and highly visible poor population. For Malthus and others observing these changes, the optimistic tenor of theoretical writings on political economy was unjustified. Instead the surrounding reality needed to be observed, counted – and accounted for. The awareness

Oliver asking for more.

Source: Illustration by George Cruikshank from *The adventures of Oliver Twist* (Chapman & Hall)

of misery in the midst of increasing wealth needed to be explained; and its theological meaning also needed to be comprehended. If this were done, Malthus argued, it would be evident that population expansion was unsustainable: that it resulted in hardship, as food became insufficient, prices rose and wages fell. Influenced by Smith's ideas on the operation of self-interest, Malthus argued that remedial attempts to deal with such hardship by parish subsidies to families were counterproductive in that they produced incentives to marry and have children, thus exacerbating the problem. In the first edition of the *Essay*, Malthus merely advocated the importance of empiricism – of systematic observation and measurement to support his argument. But in the subsequent editions (from 1803 onwards) he supported (and modified) his argument with recourse to any relevant tables and figures he could access. The use of numerical information not only to support but also to modify or contradict aspects of Malthus's original argument

> ... encouraged other advocates of numerical data to imagine that numerical information could be used to challenge their opponents' theoretical presuppositions or to defend their own, precisely because numbers seemed not always to support the thesis one set out with – precisely because numbers seemed to be divorced from theory. (Poovey, 1998, p 292)

Of course, the numbers that were available for justifying or producing an argument were few and far between; and data were not centrally collected by the state at this time. The first national Census took place in 1801, providing for the first time comprehensive population information – but little else. Meanwhile, those figures that were available came from parish records or from individual efforts that were predominantly locally based. While registration of marriage had been a requirement for the validity of the marriage from 1754, registration of births and deaths was not systematised until 1837[3].

There was, nevertheless, in the first decades of the 19th century, an increasing interest in amassing numerical data. The period saw the foundation of a number of statistical societies, with the meaning of the term 'statistics' at this time deriving from the German usage relating to data necessary to inform the activity of the state. It was, fundamentally, an exercise in the collection of 'facts' (Stigler, 1999). Findings from household enquiries might have been exhaustively counted and tabulated, but without any attempt to cross-tabulate or to investigate associations (Williams, 1981).

It was, however, recognised (for example by J.R. McCulloch) that the formation of a general knowledge in keeping with the ideas of political economy and the ability of the state to sustain and justify a free-market position required the systematic collection of national data (Poovey, 1998). McCulloch did much to popularise Adam Smith's ideas through regular reprints of *The wealth of nations* (Smith, 1976 [1776]) through the first half of the 19th century. He made the connection between the political ideology of laissez-faire, the persuasive power of numerical data and the role of the state. McCulloch's (1841) own voluminous compendium of factual and numerical data in his *A dictionary, geographical, statistical and historical, of the various countries, places and principal natural objects in the world* reveals a fascination with the accumulation and tabulation of numerical data, as well as a critical approach to its possibilities. His own discussions of data use and accuracy are linked to current debates and concerns. For example, there is a substantial discussion in the British Empire entry concerning the national debt and trade balances; while, when discussing England and Wales, McCulloch explicitly engages with still highly salient population debates, coming down firmly on the side of extensive population expansion during the 18th century[4], before appending tables from the 1801 to 1831 Censuses to show continuing population expansion. Following his discussion of (and panegyric to) industry and industrial development, McCulloch also discusses the topical issue of child employment in factories and the various justifications for it. Again, detailed tabulations of different mills and their composition of employees are incorporated as if they offer disinterested data, which supply "the inquirer with independent, and at the same time, precise and well authenticated information" (McCulloch, 1841, p v), as well as explicit support for the arguments in hand[5].

The state, however, was somewhat slow to collect and use data to formulate policy. Despite the strenuous advocacy of data collection by people such as McCulloch, it was not until the 1832 Royal Commission to investigate the operation of the Poor Law that systematic empirical investigation was used to inform (or at least justify) policy (Royal Commission on the Poor Laws, 1833). The findings reveal not only the way the existing Poor Law was operating but also the conviction of the investigators that there were perverse incentives built into Poor Law provision and, in particular, in subsidies for dependent children. The 1834 Poor Law Amendment Act, which was the legislative outcome of these investigations, can thus be seen as the first major piece of social policy that was empirically based. It was a policy directly concerned with poverty and poverty provision. But it took a punitive attitude towards the poor and was based on the conviction that the labouring classes would not work unless they were obliged to do so. It simultaneously invoked and condemned an alienated population. It therefore enshrined what became known as the principle of 'less eligibility', that is, the principle that those supported by the parish should always be in a worse (or 'less eligible') position than those engaged at the most basic levels of the labour market (see below). This principle continued to influence poor relief throughout the next century and beyond, and arguably survived the ultimate dismantling of the 1834 Poor Law in 1948. In a sense, then, this legislation justified those who feared that the use of numerical evidence to support a position would simply reinforce the arguments of those in positions of power, who would be able to employ what evidence they needed to support their position.

The New Poor Law

In 1832, amid growing consternation at the increasing cost to rate payers of the Poor Law, which had been the machinery for provision for the 'destitute' since the reign of Elizabeth I, a Royal Commission was set up to investigate its operation and make recommendations for its reform. Much concern was focused on the 'Speenhamland system', whereby the incomes of families were subsidised through the Poor Law in relation to the size of the families and in accordance with the fluctuations in the price of wheat. This early form of wage subsidy (or family allowance) was felt to provide an incentive to the poor and unemployed to have large families and to discourage independent efforts to increase income. The Commission reported in 1833; and the following year the New Poor Law was enacted in the 1834 Poor Law Amendment Act. The Chief Commissioner of the Royal Commission and the secretary of the Poor Law Commission established with the 1834 legislation to oversee the operation of the New Poor Law was Edwin Chadwick. He was later responsible for a major public health report on the *Sanitary condition of the labouring population of Great Britain* (Chadwick, 1965 [1842]). The 1834 legislation set up a system of workhouses to contain the truly destitute – whether through age, infirmity or lack of employment. Provision was intended to be both stigmatising, to deter applications, and to instil the work ethic through requiring inmates to undertake work according to their physical capacity. Following from the principle of 'less eligibility' it was intended that 'out relief' – or provision in cash or kind to those not contained within the workhouses should only be provided in the most exceptional of circumstances. Actual practice, however, varied somewhat from the intention, with about five out of six recipients receiving support outside the workhouse; and there was also substantial regional variation. Workhouses were overseen by regional boards of guardians to whom applications for support were made. Within workhouses, women and men were separated; and children, for whom some education was provided, were separated from their parents in an attempt to ensure that they did not learn habits of pauperism from them. The term 'pauper' was used specifically to refer to someone who made a call on the Poor Law. They were intentionally stigmatised by such an act and were disenfranchised as a result. Paupers were thus distinguished from the poor who could be deemed to be a large proportion of the working population[6].

On the other hand, the centralisation that accompanied the New Poor Law and the institutionalisation which characterised it – and which made it so hated – meant that the state had taken on the responsibility for both determining and supplying poverty relief, even if delegated to the local level through regional boards of guardians. It had also created an environment in which understanding of the causes and conditions of pauperism and the effectiveness of policy could be assessed. Furthermore, empirical research and numerical evidence were attractive to those who had perspectives or motivations that differed from the dominant ideology of the state and its officers.

Information from registration of births and deaths after they began to be officially collected in 1837 would become very important in the development of the understanding of environmental influences on mortality, such as Chadwick's *Sanitary condition* (Chadwick, 1965 [1842]), or the disentangling of the wide regional variations in life expectancy, and infant mortality in particular, that could still be found alongside aggregated improvements in health (Titmuss, 1943; Townsend and Davidson, 1982; Whitehead, 1987; Acheson, 1998). However, as Hendrick (2003, p 98) has pointed out, the presentation of aggregate statistics could also be used to disguise extremely high rates of infant mortality for some areas, such as areas of high unemployment in the 1930s. The collection of effective statistics on births and deaths was also to be critical to understanding the interaction between fertility, poverty and infant mortality, all crucial elements of debates about the future of the nation in the 20th century.

Weber's (1976) famous narrative of *The Protestant ethic and the spirit of capitalism* associates the rise of capitalism with a particular religious ethos and links religion to industrial development[7]. And indeed, much of the Christian-influenced literature on the poor stresses individual responsibility. But a religious background could also promote extensive philanthropy and systematic approaches to understanding and explaining poverty that were at odds with dominant ideas. This influence becomes particularly evident in the social surveys deriving from Quaker families (considered in Chapter Five) that could combine a commitment to liberalism with an attempt to understand and account for surrounding misery and a conviction of a moral obligation to seek for solutions (Rowntree, 1902; Cadbury et al, 1908; see also Briggs, 1961, pp 6-45). In addition, alternative political positions could also respond eagerly to the apparently indisputable power of numbers. For example, Engels' *The condition of the working class in England* (Engels, 1969 [1845]), an early exposition of a Marxist historical account, is crammed with figures from numerous sources, as well as detailed observations of factory workers, quotations from the statements of Factories Inquiry Commissioners and extensive citations from workers' newspapers (Engels, 1969 [1845]. The information contained in it is extensive and detailed, the argument original and the analysis compelling. Yet it is noticeable that Engels does not clearly distinguish between the quality or the type of his sources, only indicating where the shameful conditions are observed *despite* the liberal leanings of the authors. The evidence to be marshalled is therefore comprehensive rather than selective. And the argument comes to seem less a consequence of the facts than the framework within which the various facts have been ordered to support a passionately held moral and political position.

Creating the conditions for the 'discovery' of child poverty

At this period there does not appear to have been a clear differentiation between what constituted research rather than journalism or polemic, just as there was not a profession of recognised social researchers. Nor was there necessarily a greater credibility attributed to particular forms of knowledge or campaign bases. Calls to action could be based on conviction, anecdotal observation or systematic observation and tabulation. The development of a clearer social research base can be attributed to the combination of three factors towards the end of the 19th century and into the 20th century. These were:

- the development of ways of causally relating and generalising from 'facts' (the rise of statistics);
- the creation and expansion of numerous professionals directly involved in delivering social policy and with direct and informed experience (teachers, midwives, public health officials, factory inspectors and so on); and
- the development of the social survey itself.

Before all of these occurred the status of what constitutes research and its ability to draw conclusive policy implications was ambiguous. This can be seen in the journalist and writer Henry Mayhew's (1980 [1849-50; 1861-62]) voluminous accounts and descriptions of occupations. His work has been credited as being the first poverty survey, and his personal inquiries and observations have been accorded the status of the earliest English ethnography (Thompson and Yeo, 1971). The texts on which these judgements are based were a series of weekly 'letters' describing, first-hand, London occupations and their attendant wages, which were written for the *Morning Chronicle* (Mayhew, 1980 [1849-50]). These were followed by serial publications re-using some of the *Morning Chronicle* material but adding much new, which were collected together as *London labour and the London poor* (Mayhew, 1861-62). The detailed accounts give a vivid impression of the working lives of those engaged in different trades and, often, the miserable insufficiency of wages. A fascination with wages as the critical means to understanding the economics of capitalism was also an ongoing feature of research throughout the 19th and early 20th centuries. It was not only a core element of Marxist theory but also was the subject of much pioneering statistical work, such as A.L. Bowley's historical studies of wages (Bowley, 1898, 1937). Mayhew, however, as Williams (1981) has convincingly argued, was seeking to create systematic generalisations from his detailed accounts and yet, instead, became immersed in ever more detailed classifications and sub-classifications that inhibited his ability to demonstrate larger patterns or causal relationships from his material.

It was only in the latter part of the 19th century and the early decades of the 20th century that the discipline of statistics really emerged and was able to tackle questions of social investigation, including developing methods for assessing causal relationships or associations. Francis Galton, a cousin of Charles Darwin, was led to develop the concept of regression towards the mean in the 1860s through his interest in *Hereditary genius* (Galton, 1998 [1869]), even though the material which the concept was derived from was based on tabulations of fathers' and sons' heights (Stigler, 1999). Karl Pearson initially worked with Galton and went on to make great strides in statistical theory, including developing the chi-square test as a measure of association for categorical data at the beginning of the 20th century. Both were also principal figures in the eugenics movement. This common interest was not coincidental to their statistical work, but was the corollary of both trying to develop notions of statistically significant causal relationships and of systematic observation of the social world, where heredity to all appearances played an important role.

Darwin's work on *The origin of species* (1998 [1859]) and the appropriation of his theory of 'natural selection' by Social Darwinists concerned about the purity of the 'race' fed into the developing interest in eugenics (Banton, 1998). The commitment to eugenics as a principle of ensuring a sound future for the nation was widespread at the time. It covered a range of political positions and implied an equally wide range of 'solutions'. For example, Pearson shared with the socialists Sidney and Beatrice Webb, vehement critics of the Poor Law (Beatrice Webb was author of the 1909 Minority Report for the Commission of Inquiry into it [Wakefield et al, 1909]),

> a belief in the rational perfectibility of human society, a reverence for the efficacy of scientific empiricism and an acceptance that the state could and should direct its citizens in the means to improve themselves, and a meritocracy as the ultimate goal. (Szreter, 1996, p 184)

Their differences only came to light when the public outcry over the quality of recruits for the South African wars (1899-1902) prompted (reluctant) government action. Despite their common concern for 'national efficiency', Pearson and the Webbs were in fact shown to be at political extremes in discussions of policy responses. For example, the Webbs supported the extension of the franchise and financial assistance for families with children, while Pearson did not.

The broad-based strength of the eugenics movement and interest in issues of heredity increasingly resulted in a focus on children and child welfare as the critical social policy issue. This occurred in parallel with the increased importance of school boards and of the growing numbers of personnel who were directly employed in relation to social policy issues in identifying child welfare and poverty[8]. It was also exacerbated by a demographic shift that began towards the end of the 19th century. There were, from this period, rapid declines in fertility, initially among the middle classes but closely followed by the urban working classes, resulting in fertility below replacement rates being established by the 1930s. Concerns about the 'quality' of children, especially their nutrition and wider welfare, were therefore heightened by the reductions in quantity. Thus, if a major concern of the 19th century had been the increase in population and, specifically, the number of children relative to the adult population, by the early years of the 20th century this had shifted to a concern with the lack of reproduction and broader concerns about the future of the nation. Concerns for both quality and quantity could be regarded as complementary by those promoting investment in poor children and support for them, or as in tension by those who perceived the large families of the poorest classes as being symptomatic of their 'backwardness'. Moreover, declines in infant mortality, by many regarded as reflecting the increasing well-being of the nation, could themselves be read by those anxious about the quality of the nation as representing a preservation of the 'less fit' through the interventions of medical science. As Frank F. White (2001 [1928]), in an article published in *Eugenics Review*, complained,

> The number of infants and young children ... who are being saved today – at any rate for a while – is evident. But what is the *nature* of many of these children saved? In the majority of cases are they of the best stocks, or of the worst? The answer in view of the existing differential death and birth-rates is unfortunately only too obvious. They are, for the most part, physical and mental defectives who, under a sterner regime, would unquestionably have been eliminated soon after birth by natural selection. (White, 2001 [1928], pp 166-7)

Anxiety about fertility rates continued across the century, with the appointment of a Royal Commission on Population in March 1944, which reported in 1949. At the same time, the appropriateness and effectiveness of direct state involvement in family fertility were challenged by Richard Titmuss (Titmuss and Titmuss, 1942). In this period, Titmuss was continuously engaged in critically analysing social welfare and in providing conceptual positions from which to explore the role of social policy, generally, and in relation to poverty, specifically (Titmuss, 1943, 1958). His discussions of fertility and infant mortality were thus part of a wider intellectual contribution, which had a great influence on the ways that other researchers considered the role and problems of the welfare state and the methods for analysing its functioning. More recently, population concerns have focused on the problems associated with funding pensions in the context of greater longevity and below replacement-rate fertility.

The final element in creating a momentum for "a novel collectivist, interventionist language for addressing the nation's social problems, an ideology and practice of social reform" (Szreter, 1996, p 192) was the development of the 'poverty' survey. It is worth noting that what is regarded as the first poverty survey was dependent on the participation of functionaries of the incipient welfare state in the form of school board members. The systematic revelation and classification of poverty among families with children was, thus, intimately connected with the establishment of the education system, the containment of children within schools and their classification as schoolchildren. The UK poverty survey did not derive from the statistical movement, although its potential was swiftly appreciated and adopted by statisticians such as Bowley in the years after B. Seebohm Rowntree's survey of 1901. The social survey developed from a large-scale investigation of poverty and employment in London in the 1880s by Charles Booth (Booth, 1903). Booth himself is regarded as having derived his interest in basing legislation on 'facts' from his positivist Comtian background and upbringing. He undertook a major survey in which he used school board visitors to assess the poverty of the households they visited. While they only visited families with children, he extrapolated their findings to the whole population and developed a schema of eight categories of poverty or well-being[9]. He also classified streets according to the characteristics of their inhabitants on a series of highly detailed maps, and by these means implied a novel, environmental aspect to poverty. Environmental explanations had been developed by Chadwick in relation to public health in his seminal work of 1842, which made the connection between differential mortality rates and differences in living conditions across areas (Chadwick, 1965 [1842]).

Such environmental explanations had, however, up to this point tended to remain of interest primarily to local medical officers of health.

Booth's survey provoked wide interest, including that of B. Seebohm Rowntree, son of the Quaker chocolate manufacturer, Joseph Rowntree. Seebohm Rowntree's background fitted him for survey investigation: his father had himself carried out social investigations into temperance habits (Rowntree and Sherwell, 1899) and was committed to philanthropic activities and, in particular, being a good employer (Briggs, 1961). Concern for the labourer and the condition of their life was therefore a religious prescription that Rowntree had seen exemplified during his upbringing. In addition, the Quaker attitude to children and their welfare was very different from that of evangelical Protestantism, which stressed their incipient waywardness. Rowntree pursued in York in 1899-1900 an attempt to replicate Booth's London poverty survey (Rowntree, 1902). In the process, he adopted Booth's methodology in part, but also developed the notion of a 'poverty line': an allowance of income which met strictly defined minimum needs and therefore below which a family was undeniably in poverty, regardless of how they actually spent their income. This methodological innovation enabled Rowntree to demonstrate that poverty was (or could be) a consequence of lack of money rather than of dissolute behaviour. Although this claim did not go uncontested, Rowntree's poverty line and its clear linking of income and poverty was the final element in a process of the development of a certain commitment to state action.

Acknowledgement of crucial 'facts', when presented in ways which combined statistical advances in sampling and in measurements of association with systematic forms of collection, became much more likely. Political conditions still needed to be favourable to the actual enactment of policy, and there was little possibility of action that overturned countervailing preoccupations. Nevertheless, the methods of persuasion in the 20th century began to take on a form more immediately recognisable as 'research' and more susceptible to acknowledgement as such by the state.

Such research still combined the twin aspects of observation and counting that Malthus had so controversially emphasised – but not necessarily in the same directions. The social survey, as pursued by statisticians such as Bowley, had a tendency to become a demonstration of the possibilities of sampling and generalisation as it moved away from meaningful poverty lines (Bowley and Burnett-Hurst, 1915; Bowley and Hogg, 1925). On the other hand, the interactive observational strand of Mayhew's work was sustained by such studies as the Fabian Women's Group's investigation of life among 'respectable' but highly stretched working-class wives in the period 1909 to 1913. In this study it is impossible to identify, for example, the sample size (Pember Reeves, 1979 [1913])[10]. However, the work is full of detail that conveys not only the vivid reality of the women's lives but also their relationship with the 'investigators' who visited them and collected the information from their budgets. The power of observation was perpetuated in future decades by works such as Orwell's *The road to Wigan Pier* (Orwell, 2001 [1937]), and continued in the post–Second World War period in ethnographic studies such as Michael Young and Peter Willmott's 1957 study of East End kinship networks (Young and Willmott, 1986).

Campaigning around child poverty: the role of research

Those campaigning for specific social policy changes would draw on both observational and statistical research as a means of creating a persuasive argument. Campaigners would also employ sentimentality about children and their acknowledged vulnerability when campaigning around child welfare. This sentimentality and the recognition of children's greater vulnerability to hardship were crucial to the development of child poverty policy. However, there was also increasing acknowledgement of the need to demonstrate relationships and to argue from research findings. Eleanor Rathbone, for example, in her tireless (but resisted) campaigning for family endowment, utilised both vivid impressions of women's lives and the latest evidence from surveys and administrative data, as well as international comparisons (Rathbone, 1924). The arguments in favour of family endowment were persuasive and convinced many influential persons, including the economist John Maynard Keynes, and William Beveridge, the architect of post-war social insurance and social assistance. Nevertheless, the persuasion was resisted at government level as long as economic and political argument rendered family allowances inexpedient.

While research on child poverty appears to have made little impact following the developments under the liberal governments preceding the First World War, the period immediately following the Second World War has often been viewed as a time of consensus (Glennerster, 1995), when the welfare of the population, including (and perhaps especially) the welfare of children, was seen as inviting wide public support and broad endorsement from all the main political parties. The welfare state settlement arising from the consensus was perceived as being both a demonstration of the commitment to the welfare of the population and to have provided a solution to the issue of poverty and child deprivation in particular. Following a second social survey of York in 1936, Rowntree repeated his investigation once more in 1950 (with the assistance of Lavers) and seemed to confirm the optimistic perspective: the third poverty survey indicated that poverty had massively reduced since the mid-1930s and that this was largely as a consequence of the changes in social policy (Rowntree and Lavers, 1951). As far as poverty remained, it seemed to be a problem for older people (particularly single older people) rather than children.

However, not only were there problems both with the calculations and the methodology of the survey (Atkinson et al, 1981); in addition, the developments were not necessarily sustained. Thus, it gradually became apparent that:

• the major beneficiaries of the welfare state had been the middle classes;
• economic pressures were undermining or failing to increase the value of benefits;
• low wages could mean out-of-work benefits were greater than earnings in work, resulting in the imposition of the 'wage stop' to limit out-of-work benefits in line with in-work expectations of earnings; and
• poverty was far from extinct.

Researchers now began to use existing government surveys for the explicit measurement of poverty and to ascertain its trends. The Ministry of Labour regularly conducted a survey on budgets to establish the rate of the retail price index. It began to be recognised that the data collected in such a survey could be used for other purposes as well. The particular survey carried out in 1953/54 was not only much larger than previous surveys, but in addition, the Ministry expressly indicated that it might prove valuable for forms of social investigation outside its explicit use for the retail price index (Abel-Smith and Townsend, 1965). Poverty researchers took advantage of this potential, including its possibilities for making direct comparisons of change over time, and in 1965 Abel-Smith and Townsend published their investigation of poverty comparing the years 1953/54 and 1960. The secondary analysis of government-based and other surveys for the investigation of income and poverty and their change over time is now commonplace among social researchers. Specially designed surveys continue to have a role; but even then they may be related to large-scale, repeated cross-sectional government surveys, in the use of some comparable questions or in their sampling frames. The number and availability of large sample surveys of the population have been critical in the understanding and development of research into poverty in general and child poverty in particular.

The analysis of poverty and welfare state provision carried out not only by Abel-Smith and Townsend, but also by Tony Lynes (1962), Dorothy Wedderburn (1962) and Richard Titmuss (1958), led to the reassertion of the connection between academic research and campaigning with the formation of the Child Poverty Action Group (CPAG) in 1965. All these researchers were associated with CPAG, as were later influential researchers such as Ruth Lister and Fran Bennett[11]. The work of these and others heavily committed to child poverty research and policy analysis has crossed decades in which approximately alternating Labour and Conservative administrations gave way to an extended period of Conservative rule from 1979-97. This was followed by a Labour landslide in 1997, which has now gone into its second term. While economic anxieties were a feature of approaches to social security during both Labour and Conservative terms up to 1979, the subsequent period of 1979-97 has been seen as marking a particularly strenuous approach to welfare state reduction, alongside a commitment to monetarism on the economic side and to an emphatic form of liberal individualism on the ideological front. In fact, while the dismantling of the welfare state was never achieved in the way that had been intended (Pierson, 1994), and welfare state spending increased, the period was marked by a particularly punitive approach to unemployed people (and therefore their families), and poverty was neither acknowledged nor inequality accepted as problematic by the Conservative administration. The legacy of the Thatcherite era continued to be felt in the pervasive political and public language of individualism, in the acceptance of marketisation and competitiveness within welfare state institutions and in the 'naturalisation' of inequality, with a focus within the subsequent Labour government on equality of opportunity rather than equality of outcome. Continuities with much more longstanding preoccupations have also been observed in the post-1997 period, with continuing anxiety about national competitiveness, about the role of families in perpetuating disadvantage, and about the importance of children as a national asset requiring investment.

The creation of a policy agenda?

Nevertheless, the period since 1997 has also displayed shifts in attitudes both among the public and among policy makers, including a remarkable public acknowledgement of poverty and the responsibility to do something about it. As Robert Walker pointed out:

> Before 1 May 1997, poverty had been a proscribed work in official circles for a political generation and the idea that government should or, indeed, could, do anything to eradicate it was ridiculed. Tony Blair not only promises to eradicate child poverty, he commits himself to a

---

timetable that could conceivably fall within an unbroken spell of Labour rule. (Walker, 1999a, p 139)

Government expenditure on children since 1999, both through education spending and in child-related benefits, has shown large increases. And children have been placed explicitly at the centre of a policy agenda that emphasises the damaging impacts of deprivation, and the unacceptability of ignoring child poverty. The Chancellor of the Exchequer, Gordon Brown, has repeatedly referred to child poverty as 'a scar on the soul of Britain' (in speeches throughout 2000 and 2001), and accompanied this view with a systematic strategy for improving the incomes of the poorest families with children. Moreover, the availability of data resources for researchers in the fields of deprivation and poverty has expanded, and there would seem to be greater engagement between government and the research and lobbying community – although on whose terms is a thornier issue[12].

Throughout this period of political and ideological shifts from 1979, David Piachaud and Jonathan Bradshaw emphasised the recognition of child poverty and the inadequacy of state policies in responding to it. Their demonstrations of the inadequacy of state support included a return to 'budget standards' investigations, where estimates of needs are compared to rates of benefit or allowances. Piachaud revived the budget work of the early social surveys in his work on *The cost of a child* (Piachaud, 1979). Here he paralleled the use that Rowntree originally made of budget standards to challenge dominant assumptions (in this case about the adequacy of Supplementary Benefit allowances for children rather than about the adequacy of wages). Budget standards work was subsequently pursued by both Bradshaw (1993) and Hermione Parker (1998). The effectiveness of the welfare state was also challenged by studies that illustrated the extent of non-take-up of benefits for which people were apparently eligible. Abel-Smith and Townsend drew attention to the numbers who were living below different multiples of national assistance levels in their 1965 study, highlighting a number of reasons. Subsequent studies have focused on issues of non-take-up specifically (Kerr, 1983; Falkingham, 1986; Dorsett and Heady, 1991; Fry and Stark, 1993; Craig, 1991). Coming from a different angle in judging policy effectiveness, Holly Sutherland and David Piachaud have evaluated the aims of the government since 1997 to reduce child poverty and the effectiveness of the policies put in place to achieve this using microsimulation methods, which can compare child poverty scenarios in which tax and benefit changes are not implemented, with those in which they are (Piachaud

Name of Householder	Mr.XYZ				

Name of Householder Mr.XYZ

Street and Number 22 Lake Success Terrace

Rent } £1.2s.9d.
Rates }

Total number of occupants 8 (including lodger)
Number of rooms 6
Bathroom (Yes or No) Yes

Members of Household and status.	Age.	Sex.	Occupation and where employed.	Wage.
Mr.XYZ	57	M	Railway Worker	£5.19s.6d.
Mrs.XYZ	50	F	Housewife	
Daughter	18	F	Packing Dept.of -- & Co }	
Daughter	17	F	Packing Dept.of -- & Co }	£2. 5s.0d.
Daughter	15	F	Open-Air School. Value of School milk	2s.3d.
Son	9	M	School Family allowances	10s.0d.
Son	8	M	School Value of vegetables grown	2s.6d.
Mr.ABC. (Lodger)	31	M	Bus Driver Paid by lodger	£1.10s.0d.

(Say if children are at school, and if 15 or over and unemployed, if they are attending any classes).

Do the children receive free School meals? No; pay 2s.6d.each per week

Do the children receive free milk (a) at School? Yes

(b) in holidays? No

Amount paid by each child in employment for board and lodging Eldest 25s. a week;Second 20s.

Amount paid by lodgers 30s. a week

Amount received from sub-tenants not boarded None

Sums received for:—

Unemployment Insurance None

National Assistance (i.e. "Public" Assistance) None

Health Insurance None

Sick Clubs None War Pension None Widow's Pension None

Old Age Pension (including supplementary) None

Are all/meat/some of vegetables consumed home grown? Yes - some

GENERAL OBSERVATIONS ON HOUSEHOLD:- A modern council house. The family have not really recovered from four years' continuous unemployment 1934-37. Buying furniture on instalment system (15s.9d.) per week. Complained of high cost of children's clothes and poor quality of shoe leather.

Source: Taken from *English life and leisure*, Rowntree and Lavers (Longmans, Green and Co, 1951)

and Sutherland, 2001; Sutherland and Piachaud, 2001; Sutherland et al, 2003).

At the same time, Ruth Lister, among others, has continued to stress the relationship between women's and children's welfare (for example, Good at al, 1998). This issue has gained increased impetus from the rising numbers of lone-parent families which are predominantly female-headed, and the consequent policy and academic attention paid to them (Bradshaw and Millar, 1991; Ford and Millar, 1998; Lewis et al, 1998; Rowlingson and McKay, 2001). Attention to budgeting that can be seen as a modern descendant of the Fabian women's group study and of the Spring Rice (1981 [1939]), Pilgrim Trust (1938) and M'Gonigle and Kirby (1936) studies of the 1930s can be found in Morris's (1984) exploration of arrangements for managing income within unemployed households, with the insights also into intra-household distributions that that brings (see also Morris, 1990). There has also been an on-going strand of research perpetuating a commitment to recognising and understanding how poverty is experienced by families themselves (for example, Kempson et al, 1994; Kempson, 1996), including the ways that mothers provide for their children in straitened circumstances (Middleton et al, 1994; see also Middleton et al, 1997); and Ridge (2002) has espoused a child-centred approach, which asks children in low-income families themselves about their experiences, the better to understand what being a poor child actually means.

The interrogation of the effectiveness or operation of benefits (and their appropriateness as measures of poverty or 'poverty lines') was accompanied by ongoing debates and discussions about what poverty actually meant and what that implied for appropriate (and inappropriate) definitions. Increasingly, this discussion polarised on the question of whether poverty was 'absolute' or 'relative'. Townsend had made a strong case in his 1979 study of *Poverty in the United Kingdom* for the acceptance of an understanding of poverty based on people's inability to participate in the society of which they formed a part. While his method received substantial criticism (Piachaud, 1981), his argument about the importance of participation was influential. In making this argument he set himself in opposition to the 'traditional' form of poverty survey, as expounded by Rowntree, claiming that such 'absolute' understandings of poverty were inappropriate for thinking about how people were prevented or enabled through their circumstances from leading a 'normal' life. In fact, Townsend was setting up something of a straw man in the case of the 'absolute' measures he was opposing himself to (Townsend, 1985; Veit-Wilson 1986a, 1986b); but while a 'relative' definition of poverty is widely accepted as appropriate (and endorsed by the government's own *Households Below Average Income* series, which explores the composition of those living below various fractions of average income), the concern that the standards of living implied by such measures may not reflect what we intuitively understand to be poverty has continued. Amartya Sen's contribution to the debate in speaking of absolute capabilities that are defined relatively has not tended to resolve the arguments or to diminish concerns that estimates of poverty may become an artefact of the measure itself and the fact that it is linked to a moving reference point (Sen, 1983, 1985, 1987).

If the challenge at the beginning of the 20th century was to demonstrate that poverty was about insufficient income, the challenge for researchers towards the end of the century became to demonstrate what income poverty meant in terms of experiences, or what would constitute an adequate or decent standard of existence. Thus, Mack and Lansley (1985) pursued Townsend's insight into participation but attempted to take it one stage further by finding a socially-endorsed measure of what people should be able to expect in terms of their standards of living, thus dealing with the argument that poverty definition necessarily retained an 'expert' aspect. In the most recent example of this work, measures for what constituted a reasonable standard of living specifically for children were also included (Gordon et al, 2000).

The research on 'consensual' measures of poverty is also part of a broader development, building on Townsend's (1979) study, which has argued that income is simply a proxy for poverty (Ringen, 1988) rather than a measure of poverty itself; and that poverty needs to be measured through deprivation measures that explicitly say something about people's experience rather than their current income level (which may not reflect much about their spending – or about their spending on their children) (Callan et al, 1993; Nolan and Whelan, 1996; Whelan et al, 2001). Although measures of deprivation have a number of problems, including being unclear in the rationale for the quantification of poverty – or child poverty – at particular levels of deprivation, they too have had an impact on political thinking and policy. Questions about the *Poverty and social exclusion in Britain* survey (Gordon et al, 2000) were explicitly asked at a select committee inquiry into child poverty (WPSC, 2004) and material deprivation measures have been included in the Department for Work and Pensions' plans for measuring and monitoring child poverty in the longer term (DWP, 2003a). Moreover, the Department for Work and Pensions also commissioned research on which indicators should be included in its Family Resources Survey on which the measures of *Households Below Average Income,* and some of its child poverty targets, are based (McKay and Collard, 2004).

Finally, while most of this account is concerned only with Britain and its policy, it is important to reflect on the role of the international community in both drawing attention to child welfare issues and creating an imperative to further action. Since the Geneva Convention of 1924, there has been an international acknowledgement of the primacy of the welfare of the child. Such instruments, particularly when supported by comparative research indicating how well Britain is managing to fulfil the commitment relative to other nations, clearly had their place in consolidating and promoting policy for the alleviation of child poverty, as Chapter Six considers at more length.

Notes

[1] Malthus's *Essay* ran to six editions in his lifetime.

[2] This publication went into five editions between its first publication in 1776 and Smith's death in 1790.

[3] Registration was extended to incorporate still-births in the 1870s.

[4] "Previously to the revolution a hearth tax had been imposed; and the celebrated Gregory King, founding on returns obtained under this act, estimated the pop. of England and Wales, in 1696, at 5,500,000; and we are inclined to think that this estimate came very near the mark. A great deal of discussion took place in the course of the last century with respect to the progress of pop.: Dr. Price and others contending, on the one hand, that it was progressively diminishing; while Mr. Howlett, Mr. Wales, and others, contended, on the other, that there were really no grounds for this conclusion, and that, instead of diminishing, the pop. was rapidly increasing. The census of 1801 put an end to these disputes, and showed that, supposing Gregory King's estimate to have been nearly correct, the country had gained an accession of about 3,373,000 inhab. in the course of the 18th century!" (McCulloch, 1841, p 767).

[5] The fascination with the collection and collation of facts can be seen to continue into the 20th century with such works as Carr-Saunders et al (1958), itself a sequel to publications from 1927 and 1937 along the same lines. For these authors, however, the range of government and independent data sources on which they could draw was far greater. This role of summarising the current social world through a synthesis of figures from different sources can be seen as being taken over subsequently by the *Social Trends* series, a product of the Office for National Statistics and therefore an incorporation of this form of work.

[6] For the history of the Poor Laws, a detailed but partisan account is given by Nicholls up to 1860 and continued up to 1900 by Mackay (Nicholls 1898-1904). See also the informative accounts given by Rose (1966, 1972). The 1909 majority report on the Poor Law by the commission set up to investigate its functioning also contains the history up to that point (Royal Commission on the Poor Laws, 1909); while Fraser's (1976) edited volume contains articles on a range of activities that took place within and around the working of the Poor Law. For a detailed discussion of the New Poor Law and pauperism see Williams (1981).

[7] R.H. Tawney (1938 [1926]) also pursued this topic, although placing less emphasis on the necessary role of Puritanism in the development of capitalism in his discussion of *Religion and the rise of capitalism*.

[8] On the role of school boards in creating 'poverty lines', see Gillie (2000).

[9] Booth published his first poverty findings in 1889 as *The life and labour of the people in London*, Volume 1. The full survey, in 17 volumes did not complete its publication until 1903, by which time he had incorporated, in addition to his survey work, numerous additional sources of information, including the returns from the 1891 Census.

[10] Compare with the major investigation in the 1930s by the Women's Health Enquiry Committee, into the situation of working-class women (Spring Rice, 1981 [1939]). Despite a systematic approach and the collection of information on 1,250 women, this study explicitly downplays claims to scientific rigour: "The evidence collected would not be sufficient for statistical purposes, but would serve to illustrate what may be expected as the result of a more searching scientific investigation.... It cannot be claimed that all the answers given are accurate and in no case do the Committee wish to base any statistics on the result of the investigation; but this it is felt does not invalidate the findings which taken as a whole, combine to give a very fair picture of the sort of life these women lead" (Spring Rice, 1981 [1939], pp 22, 25).

[11] On the other hand, Frank Field made a direct move from the campaigning organisation to policy making itself, being the director of CPAG in the early 1970s and becoming a social security minister on the accession to office of the Labour government in 1997.

[12] An interesting example of this relationship is the Treasury initiating the End Child Poverty coalition as an independent pressure group that could scrutinise the government's effectiveness in this area as well as highlighting particular aspects or areas of child poverty for concern or attention.

THREE

A fit occupation for children?
Children and work

It is now widely recognised that the concept of childhood is a social construction rather than a universal absolute, the development of which can be traced historically and which varies across time and space (Archard, 1993; Cunningham, 1995; Hendrick, 1997). This chapter argues that child labour legislation (along with education, discussed in Chapter Four) was critical in establishing a relatively bounded childhood and a privileged status for children – even poor children – which was to make state support and intervention in other areas of child welfare increasingly hard to resist. The legislation was probably based less on the 'fact' of child employment[1] than on campaigners' mobilisation of sentiment around children combined with arguments that operated within the prevailing discourse of liberal individualism and laissez-faire. Nevertheless, the introduction of legislation and the creation of a distinct child population both rendered the ultimate introduction of state educational provision almost inevitable and created a particular constituency for wider poverty research.

What is a child?

The development of a particular notion of childhood as a separate sphere was first explicitly explored in the work of Phillippe Ariès, first published in France in 1960 (Ariès, 1962); and Ariès' unique contribution continues to be influential despite substantial criticism of some of his specific claims (for example Pollock, 1983; see also discussions in Lavalette and Cunningham, 2002; Heywood, 2001). Following Ariès' critical intervention, Norbert Elias (1994) famously linked the separation of the child's and adult's spheres with the 'civilising process'; and Lawrence Stone (1977), somewhat contentiously, charted changes in the nature of families and family roles. The historical and contextual specificity of childhood is now widely accepted. As Davin, writing of the beginning of the 20th century, explains,

> Childhood, like the family, or marriage, or adolescence or old age, is
> lived in a cultural and economic context; its character and ideology
> cannot be assumed.... In any culture or society ... childhood is

ultimately defined in relation to adulthood. Adults approach or reach adult status by leaving childhood; and frequently their adult authority is confirmed through their control or support of children (or both).... The duration of that period of dependence and subordination, however, is not fixed (not even by the biological benchmarks of puberty or mature growth), and nor is its content.... In England the transition to a prolonged and sheltered childhood happened, unevenly, between the eighteenth and the twentieth centuries, along with other long-term economic, political and social transformations. (Davin, 1996, pp 3-4)

In the development of social policy in relation to children, the state has responded to the recognition of childhood as a separate space and of children as having specific needs *as children*. In turn, the state's responses to, and interventions in, the lives of children have increased both the recognition and distinction of that separate space, and thereby the need to continue responding. So, intervention creates responsibility and thence the need for further intervention. Within the visibly poor population of industrialised England, the existence of a large body of children without conventional occupation and for whom 'being useful' had become much more narrowly limited to industrial labour was particularly noticeable and created both concern for them and fear of them. The processes of urbanisation and the creation of this concentrated poor population were connected with the major demographic changes described above. One conclusion that could be drawn from the situation was that adopted by Malthus in his *Essay*. He argued that:

With regard to illegitimate children, after the proper notice has been given, they should on no account whatever be allowed any claim to parish assistance.... The infant is, comparatively speaking, of no value to society, as others will immediately supply its place. (Malthus, 1992 [1803], pp 263-4)

Yet the failure fully to realise such draconian proposals, alongside continuing young marriages and large (legitimate) families meant that, as Hair put it: "The Victorian era was the first in British history to find itself forced to take thought about a flood of children" (Hair, 1982, p 36). And both the occupation of this flood of children and their lack of occupation could be seen as at odds with expectations of them. Children could both be seen as too young to be engaged in adult employment and yet too old to be cared for or to be unoccupied, especially in the increasingly urban settings in which they were found, settings which themselves were expanding with increases in both immigration from the countryside and reproduction.

Hendrick has discussed the dualities that have informed understandings of children since 1870 (Hendrick, 2003). He identifies three dualities: minds/bodies, victims/threats and normal/abnormal; and argues that these dualities formed the two sides of an approach which combined to control and objectify childhood. While all these are relevant to understanding the relationship between research into poverty, and the development of economic support for families with children, the duality of victims and threats is perhaps particularly pertinent (see also Daniel and Ivatts, 1998). As Hendrick writes:

> It is important for a proper understanding of social policy in relation to children (and adolescents) that we recognise just how much of so-called protective legislation has been concerned with their presence as threats rather than their suffering as victims. Indeed, more often than not, the image of young people as threats has undermined their reality as victims. (Hendrick, 2003, p 7)

At the same time, however, as the coercive aspects of social policy limited the freedoms of children (particularly working-class children) and consolidated their dependent status, agents of 'reform' could experience a genuine imperative to care and help. Thane (1996) has illustrated just how pervasive the spirit of philanthropy was within Victorian society.

Source: Taken from *Poverty: A study of town life*, B.S. Rowntree (Macmillan, 1902)

Nevertheless, Hendrick's point is well made. Such dualities can be seen as reaching back to the debates over factory legislation. Delinquency and neglect were not distinguished; and poverty was not a cause for concern in its own right but rather a symptom of degradation and out of keeping with an orderly and recognisable transition from docile child to regular worker. Both employment and vagrancy contradicted this order. Moreover, the current state of children was regarded as having implications for the future: undisciplined and deprived children were seen as a threat to the future welfare of the nation and its possibilities for progress. The provision of structured occupation and 'appropriate' training in schools was an obvious response to both the pathetic sight of children trooping to the mills in northern towns and the fearsome sight of ragged children filling the streets of London at all times of day or night. In so doing, it served to separate the sphere of childhood yet more conclusively from that of adulthood, putting at ever higher ages the expectation that children could contribute to their own maintenance, and bringing with it new imperatives for the state to contribute to their support.

Traditionally, the boundaries of childhood were established by custom and the situation of the child rather than by specific age. They also varied from place to place and according to the issue at hand. The situation paralleled that which Illich has described, where:

> In the Andes, you till the soil once you have become 'useful'. Before that, you watch the sheep. If you are well nourished, you should become useful by eleven, and otherwise by twelve. (Illich, 1971, p 27)

Custom and status continued to be important in defining the limits of childhood; yet the growth of state intervention increasingly required simpler ways of identifying who was referred to by legislation. Protective intervention, educational provision and financial subsidy all tend to require ages to be identified at which the individual is a child and so is subject to the particular policies deemed to apply to children. At the same time, as Davidoff et al have illustrated, at the end of the 19th century the different boundaries between adulthood and childhood could work in contradictory directions for two teenage girls – servant and middle-class daughter – living in the same household:

> A girl of 14 or 15, her undernourished body still far from puberty, was expected to do a full day's work, to put her hair up and lengthen her skirts. Yet she might be living under the same roof as the daughter of the house, of a similar age but still regarded as a child in the schoolroom, hair down her back, skirts still only to the knee, yet

physically tall, well built and most likely past first menstruation. (Davidoff et al, 1999, p 169)

We find, therefore, both research and legislation increasingly attempting to demarcate not only the end of childhood but also different points within it (for example, infancy, childhood, youth), using a combination of arguments based on convention, physical characteristics and pragmatism. Such ages then mark out what a child is, and take on the characteristics associated formerly with rather more nebulous age ranges. Thus, we find, for example, the Royal Commission that advised the government on the 1819 Factory Act attempting to legitimate a particular age for the end of childhood by stating that,

> In general at or about the fourteenth year young persons are no longer treated as children; they are not usually chastised by corporal punishment, and at the same time an important change takes place in what may be termed their domestic condition. For the most part they cease to be under the complete control of their parents and guardians. They begin to retain a part of their wages. They frequently pay for their own lodging, board, and clothing. They usually make their own contracts, and are, in the proper sense of the words, free agents. (quoted in Cunningham, 1995, p 140)

The attention to restricting the employment of children meant that state intervention had to be legitimated and that the process of such legitimation, sanctioned by the particular nature and status of children, justified further state intervention. It also meant that the identification of what constituted a child had to be considered. Disentangling the legal and social status from the biological was then, as now, deeply problematic. In both of these processes the role of researchers and campaigners would be important: they could put forward justifications for intervention while using the access that such intervention offered to more clearly specify and define the needs and nature of childhood. Critically, in the quotation above, we see that one of the determining features of what separates a child from an adult or at least a young person is the issue of the point at which they can be considered a 'free agent'. This highlights the relevance of the dominant laissez-faire ideology to the development of social policy in Britain over the 19th and into the 20th centuries. Indeed, this ideology still informed much political thinking at the time of the establishment of the British welfare state in the late 1940s.

Limiting child labour, delimiting childhood

State intervention marks out the boundaries of childhood in relation not only to age but also to physical space. The beginning of intervention in factory and labour legislation took the state down the road of demarcating a constituency of (poor) children whose welfare would be subject both to increasing interest and increasing intervention, and whose access to spaces outside the schoolroom would be increasingly strictly defined. The first Factory Act that attempted to limit the labour of children was that of 1802, which was aimed at apprentices in textile mills. A further Act followed in 1819, which prohibited children under nine years old from working in cotton mills. It is not possible, however, to observe a single point at which the differentiation of children from adults begins; and to claim that there was no sense of children as distinct and distinctly vulnerable at the beginning of the period under consideration would be an overstatement. The mobilisation of public campaigning for factory legislation around the plight of children demonstrates that they already occupied a differentiated status in the public mind, even as the extent and nature of the work they were engaged in denied that this was a universally held attitude.

The campaign for child labour legislation also interestingly reveals the ideas concerning the set of circumstances under which intervention could be justified. The campaign for the restriction of child labour was the form taken by a campaign for a 10-hour day. This campaign was associated in particular with Richard Oastler, who employed persuasive language and the fruits of his own observation and experience as a working man to conduct a long and energetic campaign (Oastler, 1984 [1830]). This campaign was little based on what we would now deem to be empirical research – but, as Chapter Two showed, such 'research' still had an ambiguous status and content at this time. For example, Engels' account of the pitiful (and, in his view, corrupting) conditions prevailing in factories in the 1840s draws on the words of factory commissioners investigating and reporting back; but equally he cites statements from polemical 'letters' published in popular newspapers (Engels, 1969 [1845]). He expresses a position in which sentiment, political persuasion and sources interact in a reinforcing system in which the ills of the factory employment of children become self-evident even to those who support child labour:

> And when one reads of the barbarism of single cases, how children are seized naked in bed by the overlookers, and driven with blows and kicks to the factory, their clothing still over their arms, how their sleepiness is driven off with blows, how they fall asleep over their

work nevertheless, how one poor child sprang up, still asleep, at the call of the overlooker, and mechanically went through the operations of its work after its machine was stopped; when one reads how children, too tired to go home, hide away in the wool in the drying-room to sleep there, and could only be driven out of the factory with straps; how many hundreds came home so tired every night, that they could eat no supper for sleepiness and want of appetite, that their parents found them kneeling by the bedside, where they had fallen asleep during their prayers; when one reads all this and a hundred other villainies and infamies in this one report, all testified to on oath, confirmed by several witnesses, deposed by men whom the commissioners themselves declare trustworthy; when one reflects that this is a Liberal report, a bourgeois report, made for the purpose of reversing the previous Tory report and rehabilitating the pureness of heart of the manufacturers, that the commissioners themselves are on the side of the bourgeoisie, and report all these things against their own will, how can one be otherwise than filled with wrath and resentment against a class which boasts of philanthropy and self-sacrifice, while its one object is to fill its purse. (Engels, 1969 [1845], p 194)

Instead of clear-cut research backing, the campaign for factory legislation had a broad base of philanthropic, sentimental and pragmatic support. It both made calls to sympathy for the vulnerability of the child and attempted to distinguish what made the child's status particular, in order to achieve a reduced working day (Fraser, 1984). Mobilisation around children was, therefore, used to attempt to force a restriction in working hours across the board.

To make his case, Oastler used the press, which was much more an organ of popular debate than it is today. In his most famous 'open letter', he employed the language of slavery alongside an emotive account of the plight of small children to create an argument designed to both rouse public outrage and appeal to the principles of laissez-faire. By those committed in other respects to the ability of the free market to adjust itself, it was assumed, as far as it was considered, that adult wages would adjust to the removal of a cheap 'secondary' labour force. Restriction of the labour of those not free to sell it would, therefore, ensure the more effective working of the market for those who *were* free to sell their labour. Oastler traded on such beliefs as follows:

Thousands of our fellow-creatures and fellow-subjects, both male and female, the miserable inhabitants of a Yorkshire town … are this very moment existing in a state of slavery, more horrid than are the victims of that hellish system 'colonial slavery'....

Thousands of little children, both male and female, but principally female, from seven to fourteen years of age, are daily compelled to labour from six o'clock in the morning to seven in the evening, with only – Briton, blush while you read it! – with only thirty minutes allowed for eating and recreation. Poor infants! Ye are indeed sacrificed at the shrine of avarice, without even the solace of the negro slave; ye are not more than he is, free agents; ye are compelled to work as long as the necessity of your needy parents may require, or the cold-blooded avarice of your worse than barbarian masters may demand! Ye live in the boasted land of freedom, and feel and mourn that ye are slaves, and slaves without the only comfort which the negro has. He knows it is his sordid, mercenary master's interest that he should live, be strong and healthy. Not so with you. You are doomed to labour from morning to night for one who cares not how soon your weak and tender frames are stretched to breaking ... your soft and delicate limbs are tired and fagged, and jaded, at only so much per week, and when your joints can act no longer, your emaciated frames are instantly supplied with other victims, who in this boasted land of liberty are HIRED – not sold – as slaves and daily forced to hear that they are free. (Oastler, 1984 [1830], pp 244-5)

Here, the radical, the sentimental, and an appeal to the fundamentals of liberal philosophy are carefully orchestrated in a public document. Oastler's contribution was a major component of a wider coalition of interests around the introduction of limitations on child labour, which resulted in further Factory Acts in 1833, 1844 and 1874. These Acts marked out restricted working hours for 9- (and later 8-) to 13-year-olds and more limited restrictions for those aged 14-18, establishing defined periods of infancy, childhood and youth. These public policy interventions can be seen as protective ones: protecting what was seen as the dependent statuses of infant (eight years and under), child (9-13) and young person (14-18) from labour excessive to those statuses, rather than creating provision for the mitigation of poverty and deprivation as such. The double-edged nature of 'protection' and the possible implications for those thus protected can be seen in the debates between those campaigning on behalf of women, where there was an argument that protection simply reinforced their dependence and made them more subject to control (Lewis, 1984). In this light it is worth noting the emphasis that Oastler pays to the sex of the children, indicating that girls' need for (moral and physical?) protection could be particularly persuasive.

Factory legislation and controls on the employment of children

There were Acts restricting or regulating the labour of children in 1802, 1819 1833, 1844, 1847, 1850, 1867, 1874, 1878 and 1891. There were also agricultural child labour Acts of 1867 and 1873, which forbade employment of children under 8.

The 1802 Health and Morals of Apprentices Act regulated the conditions of apprentices in woollen and cotton mills; and in 1819 Peel's Act prohibited the labour of children under nine in cotton mills and restricted the hours of those aged 9 and over to 12 hours.

The 1833 Factory Act applied only to textile manufacture. It established a working day for these factories as running from 5.30am to 8.30pm, with no night working for those under 19. Those aged 13-18 were restricted to working 12 hours and those aged 9-12 to nine hours.

The 1844 Factory Act was associated with an attempt to establish a regular working day for all. It reduced the hours of work for children between 8 and 13 to 6.5 per day. Older children (and women!) were restricted to 12 hours a day Monday to Friday and 9 on Saturday. It also introduced regulations about the conditions of factories.

The 1847 and 1850 Acts strengthened the 1844 Act, which had allowed for relay working (successive shifts over the full extent of the 5.30am-8.30pm period), to finally create a regular working day; while the 1867 Act extended the range of manufacturing enterprises covered by the protective legislation.

In 1874 the minimum age for all half-time employment was raised to 10 (from 8), and for full-timers to 14 (it had been 13 since 1833).

The 1878 Act was an act of consolidation of preceding legislation establishing the length of the factory working day and the hours to be worked[2]. In 1891 the minimum age for half-time employment was raised to 11.

For some, even if the removal of young children ('infants') from factories seemed justified, the continued employment of children could be regarded as serving a number of purposes in ensuring their appropriate development. McCulloch's dictionary of 1841 contains the following observations that seem to go somewhat beyond the heading of 'Health of persons employed in factories', as he engages in the debate and promotes a position not without adherents in subsequent generations:

> Children, that is, young persons, between the ages of 9 and 14 years, as well as adults, are largely employed in factories; and while the health and morals of the latter are said to suffer severely, the former have been described as being stunted in their growth, and rendered decrepit and miserable for life, by the prolonged confinement, drudgery, and ill treatment to which they are exposed. These representations of the injurious effects of what has been called white slavery were embodied in a Report of a Committee to the House of Commons, in 1832. We believe, however, that we run little risk in affirming that this report contains more false statements and exaggerated representations than any other document of the kind ever laid before the legislature ... factory work-people, including non-adults, are as healthy and contented as any class of the community obliged to earn their bread in the sweat of their brow.

> We do not, however, know that we should object to the total exclusion of children, from 9 to 13 years of age, from factories, provided we had any reasonable security that they would be moderately well-attended to, and instructed at home. But no such security is to be looked for. The parents of such children frequently want the ability, oftener the opportunity, and sometimes the wish, to keep them at home in anything like a decent condition; to provide them with habits of cleanliness, sobriety, and industry. Were they turned out of the factories, few would either go to the country or to school. Four-fifths of them would be thrown loose upon the streets to acquire a taste for idleness, and to be early initiated in the vicious practices prevalent amongst the dregs of the populace in Manchester, Glasgow, Leeds and other great towns. Whatever may be the state of society in these towns, we hesitate not to say that it would have been ten times worse but for the factories. They have been their best and most important academies. Besides taking children out of harm's way, they have imbued them with regular, orderly, and industrious habits, their earnings are considerable, and are a material assistance to their parents.... (McCulloch, 1841, vol 1, p 774)

For McCulloch, the recognition of the claims of 'childhood', were thus recognised as only applying to younger ages. In fact, it is interesting to note the redefinition of children as 'young people' and subsequently as 'non–adults' before a reversion to 'children' when considering issues of development more than abuse. It is also worth noting the attention paid to the effect of children's incomes on family earnings.

The boundaries of infancy or a period of childhood defined through incapacity and vulnerability and the consequent implicit expectations were, then, gradually pushed forward by factory legislation and campaigners to encompass further bands of minors. What is clear is that the boundaries of childhood in terms of age were fluid, and its susceptibility to sentimentalisation varied in relation to particular contexts, and in relation to the status or class of the children. This led to sometimes contradictory policy approaches. Such contradictions are still apparent today in the simultaneous demonisation of children as truants (and potential criminals) and the inflexible (and uncontested) policy aim of the elimination of child poverty.

The end of exploitation and the beginning of state responsibility?

For Hendrick, "… the campaign to reclaim the factory child for civilisation was one of the first steps in what might be described as the creation of a *universal* childhood" (Hendrick, 1994, p 26). The second step in this direction was the development of education, which was first introduced as a provision to provide training for children of the poor to be the workforce of tomorrow, but which ultimately came to affect all children. The Factory Acts explicitly linked the provision of education to the limitation of work, binding the two issues together. Initially it was schooling that was to be fitted into the child's working day, as the first compulsory elements of schooling were incorporated into child labour legislation. But employment was generally restricted by the gradual introduction of schooling in conjunction with employment legislation. For example, in 1875 the minimum age for all half-time employment was raised to 10, and for full-timers to 14.

Factory legislation was more important in creating the conditions for political interference in industry than for its level of impact on children's lives. While there were undoubtedly some children working in extreme conditions who benefited from the Acts, they only covered certain industries (which were gradually added to). Thus, the Factory Acts did not completely put an end to children's work. This was probably more effectively achieved by the introduction and gradual enforcement of compulsory education. Nor was child factory work, prior to control, a universal urban phenomenon or a substantial contribution to family budgets. Children may have been useful in certain circumstances, but they were rarely a financial asset to their parents before the age of around 14 or 15. While the financial burden of children increased over the 19th and first half of the 20th century, this was not simply due to the elimination of their earning power. On the other hand, agricultural child labour was relatively neglected by campaigners and in legislation, despite the fact that it was probably more widespread (Pinchbeck and Hewitt, 1973)[3]. However, subsequent legislation in 1867 and 1873 proscribed children under eight years old from undertaking rural labour.

The establishment of the principle of protection where freedom to contract could not be assumed was extended from 1844 to include women. They were perceived to be in an analogous position to youths, by being substantially under the control of their husbands. The question of whether women needed protection or simply a level playing field was a source of contestation within feminist and women's movements throughout the latter half of the 19th century and beyond (Lewis, 1984). It is certainly the case that children's and women's concerns could be at odds with one another, just as women's interests could vary with their situation. The increasing requirement on children to attend school, by removing potential child-minders and sources of support, could simply add to the weight of mothers' domestic responsibilities (Davin, 1996).

Current child employment law was effectively established with the 1933 Children and Young Persons Act. This Act restricted the amount of work children could do on schooldays and Sundays to two hours and also limited the times they could do it in relation to a 7am to 7pm day (Pettit, 1998). It also restricted the age at which children could begin to work to 13, with a distinction made between 13- to 14-year-old schoolchildren, who could only work five hours on Saturdays and in school holidays, and 15-year-olds, who could work eight hours. We see here the completion of the attempt to set out boundaries and limits in relation both to educational provision and to notions of physical development and conventional practices.

With the 1933 legislation, the limits on expectations of children and the possibilities for what was seen as their exploitation had been set. This has not meant that concerns about child work have ended, although they have tended to be more about breaches of the legislation than about the inappropriateness of policy itself. These concerns also continue to reflect the dual anxieties about the exploitation of children and the degradation of childhood and the fears for their impact on adult wages, with much recent concern coming from the unions (TUC, 1997; GMB/MPO, 1999) as well as from the Low Pay Unit (O'Donnell and White, 1998). Moreover, the introduction of a minimum wage in 1999 did not extend to 16- and 17-year-olds, even though they are above school leaving age, and the constraints on child employment do not, in general, apply to them. A minimum wage for 16- and 17-year-olds has, however, come under consideration in the most recent report from the Low Pay Commission (Low Pay Commission, 2004), and a minimum wage of £3.00 per hour (which is £1.10 less than the development rate for 18- to 21-year-olds and £1.85 less than the standard rate) will be introduced for this group from October 2004.

On the other hand, an ongoing ambivalence at the end of the century around the possibilities of work for children in low-income families, where employment has the potential for relieving pressure on family budgets, has been demonstrated in Ridge's study. Three of her respondents revealed both the damaging and the enabling potential of work for such children:

> "I did used to have a job but it was interfering with my school life so I quit that.... I want to show people that I can do well [at school]. Like some people think that I can't do well but I want to prove to people that I can do well". (Laura, 15 years, lone-parent family)....

> "I like working because I like being independent and I know I've worked hard for that money and I can go out and spend it.... I like it because I can go into town and buy a top and I think 'I've worked really hard for that'. It's not like brilliant money, that's 'cos of my age, but it's like I've got friends at work as well and well I just like working." (Amy, 15 years, two-parent family)....

> "It really makes a big difference because I have an opportunity to buy things myself ... I can do things sometimes that I wouldn't have been able to do if I wasn't working because then I'd have to rely on my parents and I don't like to do that, I don't like to do that at all." (Nell, 17 years, two-parent family). (Ridge, 2002, pp 46-7)

Education, as discussed in Chapter Four, may provide better future possibilities for such children. But if it is their present situation, their existence as children, that concerns them, then work may, somewhat paradoxically, still have a role to play.

Notes

[1] The records of Royal Commissions set up to investigate the employment of children in factories present somewhat conflicting evidence both as to the scale and severity of child employment. Undoubtedly there were highly exploitative and damaging situations, but their prevalence is harder to determine, as is the question of whether the employment of children was in fact in decline prior to the introduction of protective legislation.

[2] See Fraser (1984) for a good discussion of the development of factory legislation.

[3] The extent of child labour even in rural areas has, however, been contested by Cunningham (1990).

FOUR

Workers of the future: the education of children

This chapter outlines the arguments that were presented in favour of the introduction of state education, governments' tardiness in responding to them, and the consequences of the ultimate introduction of state education from 1870. While the conditions stemming from lack of education may be subject to empirical investigation, it is not possible to conceive of a piece of large-scale survey research that could demonstrate the need for state education in its absence. School is not simply a place where skills are acquired (and whether it is even the best place for this is not universally acknowledged). Rather, schooling also provides containment, institutionalisation and the mediation of appropriate forms of knowledge. It also, potentially, provides the means for the lower classes to access what is deemed to be 'undesirable' knowledge – to acquire subversive beliefs. It has also been widely regarded as having a religious function in relation to the care of children's souls. Then, as now, therefore, justifications for state involvement or lack of state involvement took place at the level of belief and argument. Even those in favour of pauper education were not necessarily in favour of the state providing it. At the same time, education is not a direct panacea for child poverty. In fact, in the short term, it may create it. The trade-off between child (or youth) labour and education continues to be an issue throughout the world today. However, as opportunities for labour, either among children or school leavers, are reduced, the trade-off becomes less costly. The development of educational provision and the regulation of child employment covered in Chapter Three, are, therefore, intimately connected.

The obstacles to state education

The history of state education in Britain is not a story of the translation of unequivocal research into policy. Instead, it illustrates the way in which the apparently obvious connection of childhood and school, of the identification of the child with the schoolchild, was neither necessary nor self-evident. The introduction of state education was not a response to issues of child welfare; but it nevertheless produced the conditions under which child welfare could become a subject of investigation and a source of concern, leading to the need for social policy intervention.

The increasing regulation of child labour not only increased the pool of unoccupied children who were regarded as a source of concern and potentially threatening, it also reduced the possible options about what should be done with them. If they could not be at work, and were not wanted on the streets, then an obvious place for them was in the schoolroom. A commitment to the value of education for children also came from across the political, ideological and religious spectrum, in widely read and influential texts. For example, at the beginning of the 19th century, the popular novelist and pedagogical author, Maria Edgeworth – herself influenced by Jean-Jacques Rousseau – was advocating the importance of education in children's intellectual and moral development. Her popularity was itself outstripped in subsequent decades by the writings of the evangelical Christian, Hannah More, who stressed the religious functions of education in inculcating Christian moral values. The development of educational provision, in the absence of employment, also provided an alternative means of producing a disciplined workforce. Both Malthus and Smith emphasised the benefits to the state (and the economy) to be derived from a comprehensive system of state education. Smith additionally emphasised that such a project would represent value for money (Smith, 1976 [1776], vol 2, p 305). Nor did they see such proposals as being at variance with their commitment to laissez-faire and ideas of individual responsibility and their general opposition to state intervention. Indeed, Malthus makes the connection between education and liberal philosophy an essential and urgent one. Government intervention in education would, in his argument, illustrate the very impotence and destructiveness of state intervention. The benefits to the state would be 'doubled'

> if they were taught, what is really true, that without an increase of their own industry and prudence, no change of government could essentially better their condition. (Malthus, 1992 [1803], p 278)

Nevertheless, while intervention in industry on behalf of the child dated to the beginning of the 19th century, it was another 70 years before the state took on responsibility for the provision of education. In the meantime, what education there was for the poor was provided mostly by churches, the different denominations taking care of the souls of their charges according to their particular beliefs. It was also provided through the 'ragged school' movement, which supplied basic education and containment for impoverished children. Finally, for pauper children consigned to the workhouse, it was provided within those institutions, where a fundamental element was to separate them from the supposedly invidious influences of their parents and to inculcate a moral ethos of individual responsibility.

As the ways in which children were educated and the rationale for education came from different positions and aimed for different outcomes, it is hardly surprising that these providers resisted the involvement of the state in a standardised education programme. While it has been argued that: "The fact that governments typically become involved in mass education before the development of other comprehensive services of the welfare state poses the question of why *education* is thought to be so important" (Vickerstaff, 2003, p 363; emphasis in original), it has, in reply, been pointed out that the British state took a considerable time to introduce compulsory education and was even more reluctant to make that compulsory education part of a nation-building programme (Green, 1990). The nation-building role of education which resulted in much greater and earlier state intervention in other countries (for example, Germany and France) was felt to be at odds with the principles of voluntarism and individualism that accompanied the philosophy of the day (Green, 1990). The different churches resisted encroachment on their care for children of their denominations; in particular, the non-conformists feared the imposition of a Church of England education on the nation's children. Despite the interest in education, therefore, there was considerable opposition to state controlled education:

> Concerned as the middle class was with education, it did not generally advocate those types of reform which had proven successful in other countries. With the exception of a small group of Benthamite experts and their radical Whig allies, the middle class as a whole was either luke-warm or intransigently opposed to state control of education, not only because it feared Anglican influence but because it disagreed with it in principle. Even had the middle class achieved undisputed hegemony over the political and state apparatus during this period, it would almost certainly not have developed a state education system for the simple reason that most of them did not want it. The peculiarities of English education clearly owe as much to the political profile of the middle class as to the gentry and establishment. (Green, 1990, p 212)

The churches continued to be one of the chief powers for the state to engage with up to the negotiations surrounding the 1944 Butler Education Act. Proponents of state education were equally vehement in their concern about the bias that a religious education might bring to bear[1]. For what was at stake was recognised increasingly as being of great significance. Children as a distinct and distinguishable body, who were increasingly rigidly defined, contained within them the material that would make up the next generation's adults. They were the future: a position that is still maintained in educational policy. In addition, however, the recognition of their vulnerability and 'innocence' together with their lack of agency, rendered children apparently susceptible to being moulded in whatever form their educators chose. Education of the poor was important; but what was more important was that it should not be misconceived.

Added to this was resistance to state provision from those who feared that education and the ability to read radical texts would encourage subversion and unrest. This attitude was hard to dislodge, despite strenuous (but of course unprovable) arguments that state education quells rather than exacerbates public disorder. For example, Smith explicitly engaged with this fear when he said,

> The more they are instructed, the less liable they are to the delusions of enthusiasm and superstition, which, among ignorant nations, frequently occasion the most dreadful disorders. An instructed and intelligent people, besides, are always more decent and orderly than an ignorant and stupid one ... [and are] less apt to be misled into any wanton or unnecessary opposition to the measures of government. (Smith, 1976 [1776], p 309)

Further reluctance to support a collectivist programme of education came from proponents of individualism. It may also have been that governments recognised the longer-term implications of taking on the charge of the care of the young, and the responsibility for wider welfare that the universal institutionalisation of poor children would involve them in.

Concerns about the subversive elements of education can reveal a parallel here between the attitude towards (poor) children and towards women. While appropriate education for women was endorsed by many relatively conservative writers, demands for *equality* of education for women were associated with feminism and subversive influences that threatened to undermine the natural order. For example, an energetic proponent of women's education at the end of the 18th century was Mary Wollstonecraft. In her *Vindication of the rights of woman* she wrote that:

> Contending for the rights of woman, my main argument is built on this simple principle, that if she be not by education to become the companion of man, she will stop the progress of knowledge and virtue; for truth must be common to all, or it will be inefficacious with

respect to its influence on general practice. And how can a woman be expected to co-operate unless she knows why she ought to be virtuous? unless freedom strengthens her reason till she comprehends her duty, and sees in what manner it is connected with her real good? (Wollstonecraft, 1992 [1792], pp 86-7)

Wollstonecraft's plea for education of women in order that they should be better able to avoid vice parallels Malthus' arguments in favour of education of the poor. The association, however, between provision of education and subversion of the 'natural order' continued to create further anxiety about state endorsement of education.

State education: for whose benefit?

Gradually, however, state education became inevitable. The increasing anxiety about the unoccupied or partly occupied masses of children led to an increasing acceptance that the state had a role in providing some sort of occupation for them. Cunningham has described how the unemployment of children presented the nation with a far greater problem than the exploitation of their labour had done (Cunningham, 1990). We can also find in Mayhew's vivid descriptions an association between youthful gangs of vagrants and inappropriate or inadequate education. In fact, Mayhew tried to argue that the ragged schools contributed to delinquency. However, his research was not adapted to making such causal inferences, and the argument was easily disputed (Williams, 1981). The developing ideas about eugenics and the quality of the nation also contributed to the impetus. Even the churches began to acknowledge that they could not provide sufficient education to keep pace with their recognition of the need for it.

In addition, as Britain ceased to be the pre-eminent industrial power, it was felt that it needed a more skilled workforce. Thus, pressures from a number of sources (among which disinterested campaigners formed only a small part) finally won the case against ongoing resistance. 1870 saw the first Education Act, which "established in principle the right of every child to some form of schooling" (Fraser, 1984, p 86). And the subsequent period has been seen as marking a crucial shift from the rest of the 19th century, with Thane writing that:

From the 1870s there was a discernible shift from the traditional notion that children were the responsibility of their families and that no one should intervene between parents and child: a shift associated with wider changes in attitudes towards both children and the family. The

> evangelical belief, much disseminated in the mid-nineteenth century,
> that children should be protected from the rigours of the adult world
> and educated and assisted to be morally good adults, was joined by
> the end of the century by a belief in the economic and military
> importance of building, from birth, a strong and stable race. (Thane,
> 1996, p 40)

The momentum started by this change of heart was continued, and in
1880 schooling was made compulsory for children between the ages of
five and 10; while in 1891 it was effectively made free. The 1902 Education
Act enabled local authorities to introduce and subsidise secondary
provision. Thereafter, with some fits and starts, educational provision by
the state was sustained and expanded across the 20th century, although it
remained critically subject to concerns about cost. For example, the 1918
Education Act raised the school-leaving age to 14, and advised raising it
to 16. However, cost constraints meant that this did not in fact occur
until 1972, while it had been raised as an interim measure to 15 in 1947.
The grammar schools (in which either places could be paid for or
scholarships could be given to those who passed an exam) kept pupils
until 16 to take the School Certificate. However, this meant that working-
class children who went to work at 14 could easily leave school without
qualifications. As Tawney pointed out in the 1920s, if working-class
children were not forced to stay on until 16 then they could never compete
with children who had this opportunity (Tawney 1922). Nevertheless,
despite such arguments, it still took over 50 years from the original
recommendation to make school compulsory up to the age at which the
General Certificate in Education was taken.

In fact, while the implementation of state education might have implied
that childhood was of equal value for all, the research into comparative
outcomes that it enabled continued to reveal that poorer children benefited
less in terms of qualifications and positive outcomes. This continued
throughout the 20th century, with an early investigation of the impact of
the 1944 Education Act revealing strong class differences in selection
into the (better-funded, more academic) grammar schools, as well as in
how children fared once there (Glass, 1963). Education would indeed
seem to have been more effective in demonstrating children's 'place' in
society to them than in creating a value-free period of childhood. And
class-related differences in educational achievement continued to be clearly
marked at the end of the 20th century (Smith, 2000).

Although children may not have been major contributors to family
incomes at young ages, older children would often act as child minders
to their young siblings or would provide domestic help that would free

their mothers for employment. They could also help in times of family sickness. The loss of such help through the children being at school could therefore impact on women's earning ability or effective management of the household. In her discussion of children living around the beginning of the 20th century, which draws on biographical sources and contemporary description, Davin illustrates the range of ways in which children could be, or were, usefully occupied outside school and the tensions (particularly for girls) between the requirements of home and school. As she points out:

> Compulsory school now, as when it was introduced, amplifies any dissonance between the needs of the family and the demands of society, between an ideal of sheltered, dependent childhood and a reality of poverty and stress where children's help is indispensable. (Davin, 1996, pp 6-7)

This is perhaps unsurprising, since education and work-restriction provisions were not intended directly to affect the poverty of the child. While they may have attempted to preserve the child for the enjoyment of childhood, they did not provide the means for that enjoyment outside school. The extension of compulsory school age meant that children were solely dependent on their families for increasing periods. While plans for the 1944 Education Act had originally involved the provision of grants for children from poor backgrounds who stayed on beyond compulsory age, this was not in the end incorporated into the Act. It was only with the introduction of educational maintenance allowances at the end of the century that the financial impact on families of children remaining in post-compulsory education was acknowledged. Thus not only was there an additional burden on poorer families of the increased length of schooling but there was no balancing support to complete to the level of getting a qualification.

Moreover, the options for those leaving school at 16 became increasingly curtailed and formalised in the last decades of the 20th century. And while the age of majority was reduced from 21 to 18 in 1969, the scope for independence from the family and decision-making roles for young people, particularly those without means, moved in the opposite direction over the 1980s (Bradshaw, 1990). This can also be seen in the operation of the social security system and its implicit expectations. From the introduction of Income Support in place of Supplementary Benefit in 1988, those aged under 25 received a lower rate of Income Support, whatever their circumstances, than those above this age. And staying on at school was further encouraged by a consequent loss of family income in other circumstances: the rates of payments for 16- and 17-year-olds were set as the same whether dependent or not; but because of the existence of the Family Premium, this could result in a net loss if there were no other dependent children in the family and the 16- or 17-year-old was not in school. Moreover, the failure to introduce a rate for 16- and 17-year-olds and having a lower rate for 18- to 21-year-olds when the national minimum wage was introduced in 1999 supported a similar position and reinforced expectations about family dependency well beyond compulsory school leaving age, even if a minimum wage for 16- to 17-year-olds has now been proposed by the Low Pay Commission (Low Pay Commission, 2004).

Further economic inducements for children from poorer families to remain in education beyond 16 were established with the development and roll-out of educational maintenance allowances. The financial implications of an increasing period of de facto, if not compulsory, school age had been recognised in 1944 in relation to the Education Act of that year. However, it took until 1999 for the introduction of educational maintenance allowances, a scheme of financial assistance for those children from poorer families remaining in post-compulsory education. Initial evaluations of the scheme (and the different variants of it) indicated that the payments did increase participation in post-compulsory education (Ashworth et al, 2001, 2002); and it has now, at a time when three quarters of 16- and 17-year-olds are in full-time education, been rolled out nationally, offering compensation to families for the extended period of children's dependency but also further confirming the expectation that education should reach at least up to the age of majority.

Actual status (whether or not in education; whether or not living independently), has, over the period, become subservient to normative expectations of children and young people's status, in line with the changes in employment situation discussed earlier. While the years of child-bearing may have dramatically decreased since the beginning of the 20th century with decreases in fertility, the years of child rearing remain substantial as children's possibilities for separation from their parents is put further and further back.

School also increasingly became a place where other things were done, as discussed further in Chapter Five. For example, school was a site where medical services were developed: children could be weighed, measured, inspected and even treated there and the school medical service preceded formal health provision outside of the Poor Law.

Education provision, then, established the child as the schoolchild. It also distinguished the realms of education and work. Where early factory legislation had introduced educational provision into factories, the establishment of education and the gradual raising of the school leaving age slowly acted to render work and schooling incompatible. State education also had implications for expectations of children: the skills they were supposed to have, and where they were supposed to be (in school, not on the street). It also had important practical implications for those investigating child poverty – they knew who was a child and who was not; or those measuring child welfare – they had an accessible population to study; or those investigating nutrition and hereditary influences on, for example, heights and weights – they could make comparisons across children of different social classes or across areas. Compulsory education also had implications for the income and welfare of poor families and the children within them. Finally, education provision enabled the effectiveness and impact of education itself to be assessed. But such evaluations, if they involved comparisons between classes, did not indicate that claims to meritocracy implicit within the very provision of education were being met (Glass, 1963; Smith, 2000).

Note

[1] See, for example, Malthus' statement that: "It is surely a great national disgrace, that the education of the lower classes of people in England should be left merely to a few Sunday schools, supported by a subscription from individuals, who of course can give to the course of instruction in them any kind of bias which they please...." (Malthus, 1992, p 276).

FIVE

Discovering child poverty: child poverty and the family to 1945

This chapter focuses on the development of research into child poverty itself and the policy response to it up to 1945. Gradually, the developments outlined in Chapters Two and Three came to mean that child welfare was more susceptible to systematic empirical research and was, at the same time, a greater potential source of concern. There was, increasingly, a policy imperative to respond to evidence of child poverty and hardship. This imperative continued to be balanced, however, by concerns over the economic implications of action as well as on-going reluctance to intervene either in the market or in what were deemed to be family responsibilities. The chapter explores the relationship of children to families, how support for children was seen as being an issue both inside and outside of the family context, and how child welfare was particularly tied up with and implicated in women's welfare. The development of policy that responded explicitly to the recognition of the financial burden of childhood (and the primary responsibility of women for children) is considered up to the introduction of universal family allowances in 1945. This may have seemed to be the beginning of an era in which child welfare was paramount; however, the story continued to be complicated by ideological and political concerns that had precedents reaching far back.

Debating state support for families: creating perverse incentives?

Malthus, in 1803, proposed in his *Essay on the principle of population* that:

> The clergyman of each parish should, previously to the solemnization of a marriage, read a short address to the parties, stating the strong obligation on every man to support his own children; the impropriety, and even immorality of marrying without a fair prospect of being able to do this; the evils which had resulted to the poor themselves, from the attempt which had been made to assist, by public institutions, in a duty which ought to be exclusively appropriated to parents. (Malthus, 1992 [1803], p 261)

The views expressed here – that the system of parish assistance was detrimental to society; that it created perverse incentives to labourers to produce large families which would justify them in receiving support; and that children were the sole responsibility of their parents – were to dominate the understanding of poor relief in the early years of the 19th century. They can be clearly recognised in the writings of the commissioners appointed to investigate the working of the Poor Law, who reported in 1833. Allowances paid from the rates via the Poor Law system were regarded as at odds both with the efficient running of a free market and with notions of individual responsibility and thrift. The commissioners' observations illustrate their conviction that the Poor Law created incentives to those with small property to rid themselves of it, and to those with good incomes in season to squander their earnings so that they should become eligible for poor relief. Also evident is the concern that parish labour with set returns becomes preferred to bargained labour in the market. As far as allowances for the support of children are concerned, the following quotation indicates an unquestioned belief in the inducement to procreation created by the provision of allowances for children:

> A case ... of ordinary occurrence, is that of a labourer earning 5s. or 6s. a week in the employ of an individual or of the parish. He must content himself with this wage–*if he is a single man*. But if he has shown foresight sufficient to provide against a rainy day, by getting a wife and six small children, his income rises from *five* or *six* to *thirteen* shillings weekly, *seven* or *eight* of which are paid by the parish. (Royal Commission on the Poor Laws, 1833, p 170)

For those considering the issue, the need for revision of the Poor Laws to remove such perverse incentives and to reduce costs to the parish was unquestionable. The result was the 1834 Poor Law Amendment Act, which was critical in shaping subsequent forms of assistance and their principles, as discussed in Chapter 2. Under the Poor Law Amendment Act, out-relief was abandoned for non-disabled people and allowances for children removed under the principle of 'less eligibility' and in order to avoid perverse incentives. Such was the impact of the philosophy that required the rejection of allowances proportionate to family size that it was not until 1945 that a form of support which recognised the extra costs of children and the difficulty of supporting them on a wage was reintroduced.

The New Poor Law of 1834 instead instituted a wider system of workhouses, that is, buildings in which those seeking poor relief would reside, in highly regulated conditions (including wearing uniforms), undertaking what labour they were capable of, and segregated by sex and age. Under the New Poor Law, there was more evenness of provision across areas and greater centralised control: a price that supporters were prepared to pay for what was deemed an effective response to pauperism (Rose, 1972, pp 8-9). Those who were driven to, or chose to apply for, parish assistance would not only be required to undertake labour but would be expected to be resident in the highly stigmatising workhouses, where accommodation and food would replace subsidies and where families were separated. The initial implementation of the Act was patchy, but with energetic circulars and increased inspection it gradually began to operate as intended, although less in the limitations on out-relief, perhaps, as in the disincentives felt to call on the forms of relief offered. One of Mayhew's *Morning Chronicle* letters provides this account of a young woman's experience of the 'house' from 1849, and her reluctance to use the only form of poverty relief available:

> I have this infant at the breast and another child. I lived with a young man eight or nine years. It is not in his power to make me his wife, because he has not the means to do so. I left him at different times, through sickness and distress, to go into the house. The last time I went in they were going to take the elder child from me and send it to Tooting, and another one that was suckling at my breast then, but I have buried it since. The thought of having my children taken from me was more than I could bear, and I thought I would rather starve. I went before the board. One gentleman wished to assist me, but the others were all against me.... I went out and lived with the father of the child again, and got a little work as well as we could, him and me too. I fell in the family way again, and I lost my second child. We were so poor that we were forced to sell or part with anything that would fetch a penny to get food. Several times I went to the house, but they would not give me a loaf of bread for the children. I thought I would not go in – I would sooner do anything first. (Mayhew, 1980 [1849-50], Letter XI, p 240)

The New Poor Law continued to determine the provision of relief to those without other forms of support through the remainder of the century. However, it came under increasing pressure, leading to a major report into its operation in 1909; and its effectiveness in stigmatising its provision meant that more attempts were made to provide support outside its remit. It was in a sense, a victim of its own success in this particular aspect (Fraser, 1984). It was finally dismantled in the 1948 National

Assistance Act. Nevertheless, concerns over maintaining incentives to work were retained even in alternative attempts to provide relief.

Acknowledging the reality of child poverty

Despite the ongoing influence of the principle of 'less eligibility', the idea that individuals could, through their own actions and labour, necessarily support the upbringing of their children came under increasing pressure. The pressure stemmed from the establishment of (initially highly contested) evidence that incomes even from full-time employment were insufficient to supply the basic needs of families. It also came from evidence of the poor physical condition of the working classes and working-class children, which research increasingly linked to their nutrition, especially following developments in nutritional science from the late 19th century onwards. And further concern was stimulated by evidence that families were taking steps to reduce the burden of children by limiting their fertility, with a consequent decline in birth rates. That this evidence coincided with a period in which Britain was facing military and industrial competition, and also a period in which the privileged status of children had broadly ceased to be contested, resulted in extensive mobilisation around the concerns of child poverty and health (see Davey Smith et al, 2001). However, there was little consensus as to what should be the solution to this problem, and research, campaigning and policy responses took a number of different forms.

Booth's survey of London in the 1880s revealed a high proportion of families with children in poverty (Booth, 1903). Some of these belonged to what tended to be seen as the feckless, deviant or criminal groups. But his survey also revealed the low wages associated with unskilled labouring jobs; and, more importantly, the problem of interrupted or unreliable work: he drew attention to the class of 'casual workers', deemed to be 'very poor'. The existence of trade cycles and the 'genuine' nature of some unemployment were beginning to be recognised by the end of the 19th century. But perhaps more problematic was the issue of underemployment, which could provide only a hand-to-mouth existence for the labourers themselves and was inadequate for the maintenance of a family (Harris, 1997). For example, earlier in the century, Mayhew's comprehensive and evocative study of the state of wages and employment in London had begun to alert many *Morning Chronicle* readers to the privations suffered as a result of unreliable and low wages and their deleterious consequences.

Booth's survey took advantage of the existence of school board visitors – those who undertook to ensure the attendance of children at school –

to conduct his household survey. He was, therefore, able to capitalise on both the knowledge of the relevant school-age population, necessitated through the introduction of compulsory schooling, and on the existence of a body of individuals, which had been created to enforce the legislation. Koven and Michel (1989) have pointed out how voluntary philanthropic activity, typically by women, was instrumental in shaping the welfare state and welfare state professions. Attention has also been paid to the way the direct contact of increasingly professionalised officers of social policies created both a window on the lives of the poor that could lead to further intervention, and a constituency with an interest in the maintenance and expansion of the welfare state. Moreover, in the case of Booth's study (as with those of Rowntree and of Cadbury et al, discussed later) such individuals could (and did), in their voluntary or state co-opted roles, impact on understandings of social problems and the construction of social policy through their involvement in the new poverty research.

Methodologically, there were a number of problems with Booth's survey: his attempts to extrapolate from families with children to all households was purely speculative; and his 'definitions' of poverty of household 'classes' were general descriptive categories that did not equate to specific criteria and were based on the judgement of the visitors to the household. Nevertheless, the survey made an impact on many of those interested in questions of poverty, and indicated some of the possibilities for systematic research into the issue. Booth, in his analysis of his poverty rates, was ambivalent about their causes: on the one hand he held low wages responsible; on the other he also adhered to the dominant, cultural view of poverty, which located causes within individuals rather than their circumstances; and, furthermore, he tried to incorporate an environmental insight, which had informed the geographical aspect of his method, into his observations:

> It must be admitted, however, that the relationship between the statistics of remuneration and those of poverty as tested by crowding is not very close. The discrepancies may be explained and bridged over, but they remain in many ways more remarkable than the agreement which underlies them. One thing is abundantly evident, that the full amount of nominal wages does not, as a rule, reach the home. Some proportion is either not received at all or else is dissipated in some way in a sufficient number of cases to materially affect the averages. Between these two great causes of domestic poverty – irregularity of earning and irregularity of conduct, both of which act in the same direction – it is not possible to divide very exactly the responsibility for

impoverished homes. According to the bent of one's mind or the mood of the moment, greater importance is attached to this cause or that, and the onlooker remembers the uncertainties of work or dwells upon the recklessness of expenditure, and especially of expenditure in drink. Moreover, these causes are complicated by interaction. A man is apt to drink when he is idle, as well as to lose his work because of intemperate habits. (Booth, vol ix [1897], quoted in Hay, 1978, p 56)

Booth's approach illustrates an understanding of poverty as interconnected with character at an individual level. And a conviction that poverty was not only related to character but that such detrimental character traits could be transmitted across the generations was a common belief at the time and one which continues to manifest itself in discussions of cycles of deprivation (Welshman, 2002).

One individual who was heavily influenced by Booth's work was B.S. Rowntree. Yet despite his 1899 survey of York being an attempt to replicate Booth's study in a different town, his almost intuitive grasp of fundamental methodological issues meant that he imposed a much more systematic approach on his survey (Veit-Wilson, 1986a; Hennock, 1991). His use of relevant professionals to get at pertinent information echoed Booth's, although he also made use of local workers with religious and health-based backgrounds as well as educational ones. And he also employed expert 'researchers' for all his surveys. He surveyed systematically all the households deemed to be living in 'working-class' streets. His idea of classifying streets clearly came from Booth, but the classification preceded rather than resulted from the survey. He also introduced a system of checks on the information gathered by those making the household inquiries, to verify their information. He collected details of the chief earner's wages directly from employers in order to obviate any problems of respondents providing inaccurate information about their or their husbands' wages. By his approach he was able to produce the powerful argument that incomes (including incomes from full-time earnings) were simply not sufficient to maintain children. He developed a notional standard, which represented the costs of only meeting the most essential needs, and compared actual incomes with this standard. By this method, he could calculate the numbers of those whose incomes failed to meet their 'essential needs'. At the same time, he could demonstrate that waste or poor management could not be held responsible for the situation of those in primary poverty, for whom, however frugal, there was simply not enough money to go round. He thus resolved part of Booth's quandary as to how much poverty was caused by lack of income and how much it was caused by bad habits or mismanagement through his distinction between primary poverty, where there were simply insufficient resources, and secondary poverty, where wastage and inappropriate expenditure would result in a comparable appearance of poverty.

He described what his notional income standard representing 'bare physical efficiency' actually meant in the following evocative terms:

> It is thus seen that *the wages paid for unskilled labour in York are insufficient to provide food, shelter, and clothing adequate to maintain a family of moderate size in a state of bare physical efficiency*. It will be remembered that the above estimates of necessary minimum expenditure are based upon the assumption that the diet is even less generous than that allowed to able-bodied paupers in the York Workhouse, and that *no allowance is made for any expenditure other than that absolutely required for the maintenance of merely physical efficiency*.

> And let us clearly understand what 'merely physical efficiency' means. A family living upon the scale allowed for in this estimate must never spend a penny on railway fare or omnibus. They must never go into the country unless they walk. They must never purchase a halfpenny newspaper or spend a penny to buy a ticket for a popular concert. They must write no letters to absent children, for they cannot afford to pay the postage. They must never contribute anything to their church or chapel, or give any help to a neighbour which costs them money. They cannot save, nor can they join sick club or Trade Union, because they cannot pay the necessary subscriptions. The children must have no pocket money for dolls, marbles, or sweets. The father must smoke no tobacco, and must drink no beer. The mother must never buy any pretty clothes for herself or for her children, the character of the family wardrobe as for the family diet being governed by the regulation, 'Nothing must be bought but that which is absolutely necessary for the maintenance of physical health, and what is bought must be of the plainest and most economical description'. Should a child fall ill, it must be attended by the parish doctor; should it die, it must be buried by the parish. Finally, the wage-earner must never be absent from his work for a single day. (Rowntree, 1902, p 134; emphasis in original)

Rowntree argued on the basis of his research that the working class experienced an uneven life-course of five periods alternating between want and sufficiency. He considered therefore how poverty extended over the life course, with childhood, and the child-rearing years (as well as old age) being particularly vulnerable. He also amplified his findings by carrying out direct measurements of the heights and weights of schoolchildren, made possible by utilising the developing class of professional or semi-professional women 'visitors'[1], and relating the measurements to levels of income.

Rowntree's work was influential in revealing the extent of poverty, and, in particular, child poverty; and in producing a method that could be replicated in other parts of Britain. Combining Rowntree's income and needs comparison with developments in statistical science and the principles of sampling, a number of researchers carried out similar social or poverty surveys in towns around Britain in the period up to the Second World War (Bowley and Burnett-Hurst, 1915; Bowley and Hogg, 1925; Caradog Jones, 1934; Tout, 1938; Rowntree, 1942). Rowntree himself repeated his survey of York in 1937 and 1950 (Rowntree, 1942; Rowntree and Lavers, 1951)[2]. Not only did these surveys serve to enumerate child poverty; they explicitly emphasised its importance. Their attempts to create meaningful subsistence scales also involved adapting diets for different ages of children, and once again we can see how 'scientific' and conventional notions of childhood interact. The graduation of child costs with age was combined with an acceptance of the standard points at which a change in status took place. Thus, even when initial estimates of costs were made for small, two-year age ranges, in the ensuing poverty line, and calculations based on it, costs were aggregated and simplified so that they only differentiated at the beginning (5 years) and end (13/14 years) of the school life of the child. Similarly, the basic needs of children themselves altered (and their costs changed) with developments in views on appropriate feeding and the balance needed in a child's diet: from being simply assessed as a proportion of an adult, a child came to have differentiated costs (George, 1937).

At the same time as the statistical household survey was being developed, evocations of the qualitative experience of poverty, more in the tradition of Mayhew, continued. For example, we find testimonies to the struggle to making ends meet provided by Maud Pember Reeves' account of the Fabian Women's Group's investigation into family budgets. Here, the relationship between the visiting 'researchers' and the women they were researching was a critical part of the study; and the detailed descriptions are as much part of the research as is the information on budgets that they contain. The study also reflects explicitly on the way nutritional and practical information is received within families. For example, having promoted the virtues of porridge in terms of nutritional value and low cost, they then explore the reasons why the advice of the visitors is ignored:

———

The visitors in this investigation hoped to carry with them a gospel of porridge to the hard-working mothers of families in Lambeth. The women of Lambeth listened patiently, according to their way, agreed to all that was said, and did not begin to feed their families on porridge. Being there to watch and note rather than to teach and preach, the visitors waited to hear, when and how they could, what the objection was. It was not one reason, but many....Well cooked the day before, and eaten with milk and sugar, all children liked porridge. But the mothers held up their hands. Milk! Who could give milk–or sugar either, for that matter? Of course, if you could give them milk and sugar, no wonder! They might eat it then, even if it was a bit burnt. Porridge was an awful thing to burn in old pots if you left it a minute.... An' then, if you'd happened to cook fish or 'stoo' in the pot for dinner, there was a kind of taste come out in the porridge. It was more than they could bear to see children who was 'ungry, mind you, pushin' their food away or 'eavin at it. So it usually ended in a slice of bread all round and a drink of tea. (Pember Reeves, 1979 [1913], pp 57-8)

Somewhere between the poverty surveys and the Pember Reeves study in style was a comprehensive survey of *Women's work and wages* in Birmingham (Cadbury et al, 1908), carried out by interested parties who included a member of the Quaker, chocolate-producing Cadbury family. Religious ethos, a tradition of direct philanthropy, including Sunday school teaching, and a first-hand connection with industry, which also provided the funds for the study, again provide the background for a major investigation. This study, however, focused specifically on the issue of women's lower wages, a more controversial issue even than the poverty of children was at this time.

Large families and low wages were seen as the primary culprits for poverty generally. Both the nature of the family with more children than wages could support, and the lack of wages that could support a family, were becoming critical issues for campaigning. On the one hand, the control of family size was advocated, for example, through the work of Marie Stopes, in providing extensive support and advice to working-class wives on birth control; on the other hand, there was pressure for support for families through a family (minimum) wage or through family allowances explicitly related to the number of children needing support. While for some concerned with the interconnected issues of women's and children's poverty, family allowances seemed to suggest the most effective means of enhancing family welfare, the differential wages of women and men were also of concern to the women's movement: if men could not necessarily support a family on their wages, so much less could women when they were the sole earners.

Few of those who were to have their poverty research accepted by the mainstream engaged directly with the issue of women's wages. Locating poverty in the family implied that family income was the crucial issue, and female-headed households were an apparently easily ignored form of family in such considerations. However, the Cadbury et al survey was prepared to engage directly with the implications of a differential wage structure. It emphasised the hardship and potential degradation caused by paying women less than they could ever be reasonably expected to live on.

> And the great crowd of those lower still, who just do not make enough on which to live, who are always underfed and underclothed; what of them? To all who have gone in and out among them it must be a matter of continual marvel that so many of them are so good. There is a heroism rarely seen or recognised in the lives of these thousands who 'keep respectable'. (Cadbury et al, 1908, p 180)

Despite the detailed, forceful and persuasive tenor of such accounts, they made little impact on policy, and equalisation of wages was never seriously considered by government as a means to improving family incomes. At the same time, the resistance to any action associated with feminism or operating outside the perceived 'natural order' tended, if anything, to delay or impede policy development[3].

In the period up to the First World War, child poverty became a publicly acknowledged reality, with increasing admissions that philanthropy on its own was insufficient to deal with it. The development of the social survey and its ability to provide apparently firm evidence of poverty, the increase of professionals directly involved with children and families, such as teachers, and the scandal over the inadequate supply of recruits for the Boer war, which itself tied into the eugenics movement, all tended to establish the need for a response from the state[4].

Responding to child poverty: direct intervention

Once the reality of child poverty and the necessity of responding to it had come to be widely, if not universally, acknowledged, there were two policy options for responding to it. One, which was implied by the household-based surveys and their income measures of poverty, was to find a means of increasing the amount of money available to the family. The other, which fitted better with the ongoing reluctance to 'reward' families for having children, and which was supported by many charitable organisations and workers directly involved with children, was to provide direct nutritional support to children. Each of these options was itself seen as being best attained in one of two ways. Arguments for increasing family support focused on either the attainment of a 'breadwinner' wage, or on providing a system of 'family endowment', which harked back to the days before 1834. Those in favour of direct intervention, particularly relating to nutrition, focused either on the mother and child relationship or on the child apart from the mother. Each proposal was attractive to campaigners for different reasons and had elements that made it both attractive and threatening to governments and to wider ruling-class opinion.

Direct intervention towards needy children was facilitated by compulsory schooling and by the direct access to children this offered. The fact that school was increasingly perceived as an environment in which children could be weighed, measured and their malnutrition noted also rendered it an obvious site for intervention, especially the feeding of children. There was much charitable feeding of schoolchildren by the end of the 19th century (with little genuine effort to recoup the cost from parents, even where that was the principle). The care of schoolchildren was systematised by the formal introduction of free school meals for needy children in the 1906 Education (Provision of Meals) Act and by the creation of a school medical service in 1907. The routine medical examination of children created a wealth of information that could be used to indicate the state of the nation's health and how it was changing over time, and strengthen (or undermine) arguments about the association between poverty and children's development (see, for example, M'Gonigle and Kirby, 1936).

Not only did school offer a place for the provision of welfare, it was also argued, most forcefully by Margaret MacMillan, that attempting to educate hungry children was pointless. MacMillan was a great influence on Sir Robert Morant, who was Permanent Secretary at the Board of Education during the Liberal reforms. Thus, not only did school provide the opportunity to deliver welfare to children, the view was also that the whole rationale of the education system could be undermined without such services. Educational investment in children, from this perspective, necessitated intervention in their health and nutrition if it was to reap results. Nevertheless, despite the attractiveness of direct work with schoolchildren from the perspective of accurate monitoring of the future generation and the avoidance of provision to parents, such interventions were still deemed to undermine parental responsibility and to infringe on the role of the family. The influential Charity Organisation Society

(COS), for example, objected that the provision of free meals was counterproductive in that it decreased parental responsibility (Bosanquet, 1973 [1914]). Instead, the COS argued that the only appropriate response to underfed children was appropriate investigation of the families and working with the whole family to instil better habits and to avert parental neglect. Supporting the COS's position with regard to the feeding of children, Octavia Hill stated that:

> I can imagine no course so sure to increase the number of underfed children in London as the wholesale feeding of them by charity. I myself know family after family where the diminution of distinct responsibility increased drunkenness and neglect, where steady work is abandoned, house duties omitted, all because of our miserable interference with duties we neither can nor should perform, and in no way is this evil clearer to me than in the provision of free food for the apparently hungry. (Hill, Address to the Annual Meeting of the COS, May 1981, quoted in Bosanquet, 1973 [1914], pp 255-6)

In addition, cost constraints were very much to the fore in the early years of the 20th century, following the expenses of war. Thus we see that, despite the existence of medical care and surveillance in schools, the potential to provide directly to all children within such an institutional environment was never fully exploited. Vincent has pointed out that despite the permissive provisions of the 1906 Education (Provision of Meals) Act, strengthened in 1914 to become compulsory with eligibility based on the child's health as well as a means test, only between 2 and 4% of children received school meals in the interwar period, even though those who were in families on unemployment benefits or public assistance amounted to a far higher proportion (Vincent, 1991, pp 73-4). Moreover, the provision of supplements such as free school meals and milk, as well as welfare clinics and milk for pregnant women was, as Webster has pointed out, subject to substantial regional variation, and local authorities were often least able to supply them where need was greatest (Webster 1985; see also Webster, 1982). The low level of benefits was not comprehensively supplemented by provision in kind:

> The total machinery of welfare was inadequate to compensate the poor and the unemployed for their disadvantages. Welfare services were too thinly spread and too erratic to serve more than a residual function. In retrospect many of the services give the appearance of welfare, without containing the reality. (Webster, 1985, p 229)

The experience of war, and evacuation in particular, had revealed the levels of deprivation experienced by some urban children and had demonstrated the inadequate organisation and provision in many local education authorities for such contingencies; while host parents could not be expected to fund the school meals of their guests. The war therefore created not only the atmosphere in which attention to social welfare commanded public support, but also forced some of the mechanisms to be put into operation by which that support could be provided directly to children. Initially, evacuation and closure of schools in sending areas – even if children still remained in them – caused a breakdown of many forms of provision:

> The annulment of compulsory school visiting, the breakdown of school education, involving hundreds of thousands of children, simultaneously deprived them of routine medical inspection and treatment, of the dental service, and most of them also of free or cheap meals and milk. It was terrifying to learn that up to the beginning of 1940 there were, out of something over 1,150,000 children in evacuated town zones, still approximately 400,000 with little or no health care at all. (Padley and Cole, 1940, p 97)

As Padley and Cole pointed out, the evacuation plans failed to take account of the unwillingness of families to separate:

> Only male calculations could have so confidently assumed that working-class wives would be content to leave their husbands indefinitely to look after themselves, and only middle-class parents, accustomed to shoo their children out of sight and reach at the earliest possible age, could have been so astonished to find that working-class parents were violently unwilling to part with theirs. (Padley and Cole, 1940, p 5)

In reception areas, however, despite initial wrangling between sending and reception authorities and between national and local government as to the financing of the scheme, this had been effectively resolved by the latter part of 1940, when, against a background of rapidly rising prices, central government spending, on behalf of both children and pregnant women, expanded (Vincent, 1991). Over the period of the Second World War, the number of children receiving school meals expanded dramatically:

> In July 1940, 130,000 children each day were receiving either free or paid meals. By February 1945, 1,650,000 received school meals, 14

per cent of them free, the remainder paying between 4d. and 6d. per meal. In July 1940, 50 per cent of children received milk at school, in February 1945, 73 per cent.... Many of these developments, however, had at least as much to do with the change of government in May 1940, the need to encourage mothers to work, fears about levels of mortality and ill health, the antagonism of the new Cabinet, including Churchill, towards the Treasury, as to Dunkirk or feelings of social solidarity. (Thane, 1996, pp 223-4)

Following on from these experiences, in addition to its reorganisation of the education system on apparently more egalitarian principles, including the abolition of all fees for state schooling, the 1944 Education Act made the school meals service compulsory on local education authorities and available to all pupils. Medical inspection became compulsory and the range of medical services was expanded.

The universalist principles that informed much of the Education Act notwithstanding, there remained an attachment to targeted support being the most appropriate. During the Second World War, R.A. Butler, president of the Education Board, argued that "if we are out to improve the conditions of childhood the most effective way of doing so would be to provide *free* meals, *free* milk and *free* boots and clothing for all children who satisfy an income test" (quoted in Macnicol, 1980, p 180). In fact, while such means-tested elements continued to remain part of the school environment and one part of the support to needy children, even as more universalist provision tended to be diminished, they were not to play a comprehensive role in the amelioration of child poverty. Smith and Noble (1995) have looked at the role of the school in terms of its social provision and have concluded that it has declined over the postwar period. Part of this is the shift to more targeted from more universal benefits. The provision of free milk to all schoolchildren (rather than just poor children) was ended in 1972-73; and in 1980 local authorities were no longer required to provide school meals except for those in families on benefit. Moreover, take-up of free school meals by those eligible has never been 100%. Yet the 1980s, a time when a particularly concerted effort towards benefit restrictions and greater targeting was being made, was being compared in research with the 1930s in relation to the detrimental impacts on children of unemployment and poverty (see the discussion in Mitchell, 1985, p 106).

On the other hand, the 1989 Children Act, which built on provisions in earlier Acts including the 1963 Children and Young Persons Act and the 1980 Child Care Act, included provision of direct services to needy children. According to Section 17, local authorities have a duty to safeguard and promote the welfare of children 'in need'; and a child 'in need' is defined as one who "is unlikely to achieve or maintain or to have the opportunity to achieve or maintain a reasonable standard of health or development ... or whose health or development is likely to be significantly impaired or further impaired ... or is disabled". But in fact, provision under this Section has tended to be highly targeted, and unable to impact on the lives of the majority of children living in poverty (Aldgate and Tunstill, 1995). Such later changes in direct services to needy children were themselves associated with the political shifts that came with a reassertion of individual responsibility rather than notions of collective responsibility. Nevertheless, the overall implication of legislation in 1944 was that children were valued in and of themselves, that the status of childhood was paramount.

If one way of responding to the needs of children was through direct intervention in schools, the alternative was working with mothers (Lewis, 1980). It was deemed that if the role (and responsibility) of the family, and in particular the mother, was central, then child welfare should, and could only, be achieved this way. Much of such work focused on educating mothers. As Thane writes:

> Medical officers of health (MOHs) and others were convinced that the chief causes of physical weakness and infant mortality were unsuitable feeding and lack of hygiene in the home which could, they believed, be improved by the education of mothers in child care and domestic skills. More intensively in the 1900s, MOHs and such voluntary organizations as the Women's Co-operative Guild and the Infant Health Society gave talks to women, issued leaflets and established schools to train mothers in child care and domestic skills. (Thane, 1996, p 64)

The profession of health visiting came into being at the end of the 19th century, establishing the sometimes ambiguous relationship with mothers that has characterised their work (Lewis, 1980). There were also attempts to establish a series of milk depots, which met with limited success; and mother and baby clinics also began to open in this period.

Maternity payments were regarded as a way of reducing maternal ill-health and infant mortality, where the stress on infant survival was enhanced through awareness of reduced fertility. For that reason, following campaigning by the Women's Co-operative Guild, a maternity payment for the wives of insured men was included in the health insurance provisions of Part I of the 1911 National Insurance Act. The extent of female ill-health (among women employees, especially married women

Source: Taken from *Poverty and progress: A second social survey of York*, B.S. Rowntree (Longmans, Green and Co, 1941)

employees) was also revealed by claims following the introduction of this Act. This demonstrated the large amount of, until then unrealised, illness, which had previously been simply endured. Much ill-health was associated with the negative health consequences of pregnancy and childbirth, and raised the issue of the extent to which pregnancy (or at least the last month of it) should be designated as incapacity:

> By these witnesses it is contended that there is in fact more sickness than was expected when the Act came into operation, and that the excessive sickness among married women is a common experience due to illnesses connected with and consequent upon childbirth. The evidence of medical practitioners is overwhelmingly in support of the view that the effect of the Act has been to disclose, especially among industrial women, an enormous amount of unsuspected sickness and disease, and to afford treatment to many who have hitherto been without medical attendance during sickness. (Report of the Departmental Committee on Sickness Benefit Claims under the National Insurance Act 1914, quoted in Thane, 1996, p 315)

For those working directly with mothers or with children, the relevance of direct improvements in parental income was hard to dispute, especially when supported by the escalating survey evidence of widespread child poverty, which family incomes were insufficient to mitigate. The campaigns to find a solution in an improvement in family incomes thus gained momentum. The direction of campaigning for family incomes, however, took two forms, which were regularly opposed to each other: to achieve a minimum (family) wage or to establish family endowment.

Responding to child poverty: supporting families or enhancing parental responsibility?

It is perhaps testament to the successful impact of the social surveys that support for children was predominantly (and increasingly) constructed in relation to the household in which the child lived and in terms of income assistance. Thus, the poverty of children became inseparable from the poverty of the family. Indeed, increasingly the poverty of children would not be measured aside from the levels of income pertaining to the household as a whole, so that to talk of the elimination of child poverty as the current administration does, is somewhat disingenuous, in that it necessitates abolishing also the poverty of adults living in the household (Cross and Golding, 1999).

Rowntree himself developed his innovation in poverty measurement into an argument about the need for a 'family wage' in his *Human needs of labour* (Rowntree, 1918, 1937); and reiterated this in his second York survey of 1937:

> The fact is that so long as wages are paid which are below the sum needed to enable a family of five to attain the minimum standard, there will always be a number of families living below it, and *these will almost always be families with young children.* (Rowntree, 1942, p 54; emphasis in original)

A family minimum wage was supported by (male) trades unions, and emphasised a family form whereby the wife's primary role would be childcare, and she would be financially supported by her husband. Rowntree's work on *The human needs of labour* and the campaign for an adequate breadwinner wage also justified differential wages for men and women. As Pedersen has pointed out:

> Men used support of women and children as an index of respectability, the basis of a claim to both extended political representation and higher pay…. men were owed a higher wage not because they actually had families to keep, but simply because the option of 'keeping' a wife was a prerogative of the male citizen….The construction of masculine identity as entailing economic rights over women and children was

one of the most powerful achievements of the labour movement, which understandably guarded it jealously. (Pedersen, 1989, pp 98-9)

Hence, the campaign chimed with conservative forces, apparently attempting to maintain the social order. Nevertheless, the introduction of a minimum wage still implied a radical level of intervention in industry, and was resisted by governments through fears about its impact on competitiveness.

The situation of those children living in families with unemployed adults would not benefit directly from a minimum wage. Nevertheless, the failure to ensure minimal levels of income within work had implications for the rates of support that were tolerated outside work. Children living in unemployed families represented a particular conundrum for policy makers, as the recognition of their poverty and the location of the solution of that poverty within the family was felt to be in tension with creating incentives for their parents to work and the position of less eligibility established with the 1834 Poor Law Amendment Act. If campaigners could look for solutions to low wages and large families in either a family wage or family allowances, such solutions were not necessarily going to benefit children in families without work, except in so far as higher rates of support for those out of work become possible once higher rates of earnings or income for those in work have been achieved.

At the same time as the two possible solutions for low wages were being proposed, then, the situation of children in families without a worker, although less prevalent, were more extreme. And their plight was to come into particular focus – for researchers and campaigners, if not immediately for policy makers – during the interwar period of high unemployment and also during the Second World War, in part through the impact of evacuation.

The awareness of trades cycles and the presence of severe recessions, particularly towards the end of the 19th century, made it hard to sustain the principle of the 1834 Poor Law that genuine unemployment did not exist. Instead, the problem became that of distinguishing between the genuinely unemployed and the 'idler'. There was also on-going interest in ways of undermining the development or maintenance of an 'idler' mentality, once those who had been committed to their work became unemployed. The virtues of separation were espoused through the creation of labour colonies, which removed the 'well-intentioned' unemployed from the invidious effects of their environment.

A parallel move to protect children from the deleterious character effects of living with unemployed parents was also attempted through separation.

Just as the workhouse had kept children and adults apart, voluntary children's organisations often stressed the importance of removing children from the family context, which was seen to be a potentially corrupting influence on the child – corruption, or at least degradation, evidenced by the need to call on the voluntary organisation in the first place (Ward, 2000). A more extreme form of separation was found in the child emigration movements (see Parr, 1980), and associated with Barnardo's among others. By apprenticing children to employers in Canada and Australia they would be far removed from the influence of their families and would also be in an environment seen as likely to be more conducive to a work ethic. It also physically removed the child poverty 'problem' in these cases.

At the same time the issue of 'genuine' unemployment and consequent poverty excited explorations into the development of an unemployment insurance system, modelled on that developed in Germany under Bismarck. The opportunity arose when a Liberal government came to power in 1906, which led to the appointment of a reforming Lloyd George to the Treasury and a young Winston Churchill, socially concerned and determined to make his mark, to the Board of Trade. The substantial Labour Party electoral success also gave additional political impetus to the introduction of reforms; and Winston Churchill recruited, to help him develop an insurance system, the young William Beveridge, whose lifelong commitment to social insurance was already beginning to take shape.

Part II of the 1911 National Insurance Act was restricted in its scope and coverage: it only covered those employed in certain trades and it did not pay allowances for dependants, although such allowances were introduced in 1921 with the Unemployed Workers' Dependants Act. Following the First World War, there arose the acute problem of how to manage the system once major recession hit at the beginning of the 1920s. Orwell described the atmosphere following demobilisation in which initial moves towards expanding provision took place:

> The men who had fought had been lured into the army by gaudy promises, and now they were coming home to a world where there were no jobs and not even any houses. Moreover, they had been at war and were coming home with the soldier's attitude to life, which is fundamentally, in spite of the discipline, a lawless attitude. There was a turbulent feeling in the air. To that time belongs the song with the memorable refrain:

There's nothing sure but
The rich get richer and the poor get children;
In the mean time,
In between time,
Ain't we got fun?

People had not yet settled down to a lifetime of unemployment
mitigated by endless cups of tea. They still vaguely expected the Utopia
for which they had fought.... (Orwell, 2001 [1937], p 131)

The interwar years were then racked by the problem of maintaining and
extending an insurance system when demands were exceeding
contributions.

In September 1924, the UK became a signatory to the Declaration of
Geneva, thereafter known as the United Nations Declaration on the
Rights of the Child. In doing this it formally recognised that: "Mankind
owes to the child the best that it has to give ... beyond and above all
considerations of race, nationality or creed" including a specific
commitment that "the child must be given the means requisite for its
normal development, both materially and spiritually" (League of Nations,
1924). This commitment has endured. At the same time, however, the
UK continued to adhere to the individualist principle that children are
the responsibility of their parents, and that the responsibility should be
stressed and enforced as far as possible.

This principle has been reasserted also in subsequent legislation: the
1948 National Assistance Act stated the responsibility of a parent to
maintain its children and the possibility of recouping the funds (Section
42). Parental responsibility to maintain children was retained in subsequent
amendments to income maintenance provision, with prosecution of
parents who do not support their children remaining an option. Parental
responsibility has been reaffirmed through policy more recently, with
the enactment of the 1991 Child Support Act and the 2000 Child Support,
Pensions and Social Security Act, which adjusts the way child support is
delivered. The systemisation of payments of maintenance by absent parents
to support their children through the Child Support Agency (CSA) that
came with the 1991 Child Support Act was stimulated by concerns with
reducing lone parents' receipt of Income Support and of instilling
principles of parental responsibility beyond the immediate household.
Recognition of the increasing numbers of partnerships resulting in
children, that did not last, alongside a long-standing ideological
commitment to the primacy of parental responsibility to maintain their
children, meant that, in certain circumstances, the state was prepared to

enforce the notion of family interdependence where family was not defined in terms of co-residence (as it typically had been for means testing of benefits). Although initially extremely unpopular, the principle of state (rather than court) enforcement of parental responsibility via the CSA was sustained, and was embraced by the succeeding Labour government as part of its overarching premise in relation to the welfare state (and social security in particular) of the parallel nature of rights and responsibilities (Deacon, 1999). Indeed, the White Paper, which introduced the changes to child support brought in with the 2000 Act, made this explicit in its title of *A new contract for welfare: Children's rights and parents' responsibilities* (DSS, 1999).

Social policy has thus been used, almost paradoxically, to distance the state from child support as well as to contribute to it. There is an ongoing tension between state promotion of the welfare of children and the concern that parents will not act in the best interests of their children unless obliged to. However, even such interventions aimed at re-situating responsibility for children's welfare with the parents tend to be expressed in terms that emphasise the centrality of the child's welfare in making such demands on their parents.

During the inter-war depression, rising unemployment raised cost containment concerns around benefit payments and fears of fraudulent benefit receipt. As Fraser says:

> No government of the interwar years could escape the dilemma imposed so acutely by unemployment: to throw the unemployed onto private charity would be socially and politically impossible, yet to help the unemployed might bankrupt the nation. (Fraser, 1984, p 185)

In this context of anxiety overspending expectations of parental responsibility were increased and concern with children's welfare was undermined. Despite the promises made in the Declaration of Geneva, as unemployment soared in the 1920s and 1930s, the welfare of children in unemployed families was sacrificed to wider economic and political considerations.

Rates of Unemployment Benefit and unemployment assistance benefits in 1939

	Unemployment Benefit	Unemployment assistance
Adult man (householder)	17s	17s
Adult woman (householder)	15s	16s
Male youth 18, 19, 20	14s	9s
Female youth 18, 19, 20	12s	9s
Boy 16-17	9s	9s
Girl 16-17	7s 6d	9s
Boy 14-15	6s	6s 6d
Girl 14-15	5s	6s 6d
Child 11-13	3s	5s
Child 8-11	3s	4s 6d
Child 5-8	3s	4s
Child 0-4	3s	3s 6d

Source: Adapted from Hill (1940, pp 3, 5)

Note the differentiation by gender within the insurance system – in part reflecting differential contributions – themselves a function in part of differences in wages. Note also the low flat rate of benefit for dependent children, intended to keep costs low. In the assistance system, which is notionally related to needs more than the insurance system, age is taken as being more important than gender in determining needs with a graduation from older to younger children. The amounts supplied to households under either system – and particularly to larger families – were inadequate to match any existing nutritional or subsistence-level standard, however meagre, once rent had been paid.

Neglecting children? Support for families in the inter-war years

Throughout the period from 1921 to 1939, during which the unemployment rate of insured workers averaged almost 15%, allowances for the dependants of unemployed people were kept punitively low (Hill, 1940, pp 112-17 and see Box above), despite the fact that there was no evidence of benefit dependency among the population and the problem of overlap of benefits and wages was relatively insignificant (Macnicol, 1980, pp 118,124). Various measures for extending unemployment benefits to those who would not previously have been covered took place in the 1920s and 1930s with the eventual consolidation in 1934 in the

Unemployment Assistance Board of all unemployment assistance, both the contributions-based and the means-tested assistance, which had previously been administered by Public Assistance Committees, descendants of the Poor Law Boards of Guardians. Nevertheless, the allowances for children showed little variation. The British Medical Association estimated that in 1933 simply to feed children adequately would cost between 2s 8d for a baby to 5s 4d for a child aged 12-14. Yet the allowances for children of all ages within unemployment insurance were just 2s in the 1930s rising to 3s by 1939: and calculations of family incomes showed that unemployed families would have to go underfed according to the British Medical Association standard once rent and other fixed costs were paid for. The extent and impact of unemployment on both workers and families was the subject of investigation and agitation. The Pilgrim Trust report of 1938, *Men without work*, was an extensive investigation into the extent and duration of unemployment and the ways in which it impacted on families. The report saw women's self-sacrifice as a commonplace response to conditions of long-term unemployment: "All of us were agreed that in most unemployed families the parents, and in particular the wives, bore the burden of want, and in many instances were literally starving themselves in order to feed and clothe the children reasonably well" (Pilgrim Trust, 1938, p 112). Similarly, the Women's Health Enquiry Committee (Spring Rice, 1981 [1939]) illustrated the way that mothers would deprive themselves in order to mitigate the effects of poverty on their children:

> Poverty ... increases the housewife's difficulties in relentless geometrical progression and it is not surprising to find that she takes one comparatively easy way out by eating much less than any other member of the family. By saving the necessity to plan for herself, the difficulties of the budget are somewhat lightened. Moreover, her weariness at the end of a hard morning's work, the steam and heat and smell in a small kitchen, combine to take away her appetite. To serve her family she has to be standing about a great deal and therefore finds it easier not to sit down to eat, which means that she cannot eat a hot dish properly. The alternative is to wait until the family has finished and then to sit down to eat whatever 'scraps that may be left'.

> In many hundreds of these 1,250 interrogatories the woman speaks of going without herself for any or all of these reasons. Health Visitors' accounts also speak of the deplorable extent to which the woman will starve herself in order that her children should have a little more or

that her labour should be lightened. (Spring Rice, 1981 [1939], p 157)

Earlier in the 1930s the Save the Children Fund had investigated the effect of unemployment on children's health and welfare (Save the Children Fund, 1933). As a result, they continued campaigning for an extension of school meals provision, up until the inclusion of the universal requirement on local authorities in the 1944 Education Act.

Children, then, or at least families with children, suffered because the economic, ideological and political costs of adequate allowances within unemployment were too high. More generous allowances, it was also feared, would increase the momentum for a minimum wage or at least produce wage inflation.

Allowances for children could be slightly more generous in the Public Assistance Committee rates, resulting in some concern when it was proposed to merge the functions of the Unemployment Assistance Board and the Public Assistance Committees in 1934. However, the receipt of these transitional benefits also raised the issue of distribution of incomes within households. The benefits were subject to a household means test, introduced in 1931, which was intrusive and assumed pooling of incomes within households, both of which caused deep resentment (Deacon and Bradshaw, 1983). The pooling assumptions might not be met or might be seen to be unacceptable and, in addition, households could be obliged for financial reasons to break up, as Orwell powerfully described in *The road to Wigan Pier*, his observations of mass unemployment during 1936:

> The most cruel and evil effect of the Means Test is the way in which it breaks up families. Old people, sometimes bedridden, are driven out of their homes by it. An old-age pensioner, for instance, if a widower, would normally live with one or other of his children; his weekly ten shillings go towards the household expenses, and probably he is not badly cared for. Under the Means Test, however, he counts as a 'lodger' and if he stays at home his children's dole will be docked. So perhaps at seventy or seventy-five years of age, he has to turn out into lodgings, handing his pension over to the lodging house keeper and existing on the verge of starvation. I have seen several cases of this myself. It is happening all over England at this moment, thanks to the Means Test. (Orwell, 2001 [1937], p 73)

The complexity of dealing with intra-household relations, with what households do, and what they can be (or are) expected to do, in terms of redistribution, continued to vex the policy agenda, even as it was acknowledged that the household means test was not sustainable (it was commuted to a family means test in 1941). Such issues could be particularly complicated when dealing with those whose age seemed to determine them as boys or girls, and yet who could potentially be earning. This confusion posed by apparently distinct and yet overlapping statuses, and their relationship to the construction of the family, can be seen in Beveridge's proposals for National Insurance rates. In treating the issue of payments for those with this ambiguous status, issues of entitlement and normative expectations on redistribution and reasonable 'family incomes' become tied up together. Veit-Wilson (1992) has commented on Beveridge's shifts between his consideration of National Insurance as subsistence benefit and his aversion to treating it in this way; but the perplexity raised by the issues is perhaps most distinct in the following Section:

> The unemployment and disability benefit for boys and girls is put 1/ – below the rate of dependant allowance. This will mean that 1/- less is paid when boys and girls are themselves unemployed or sick than if they are dependants and the person upon whom they depend is unemployed or sick. The difference is not a matter of great importance, but is probably right, in view of the fact that boys and girls of this age will be living with older people and while those older people have earnings can be maintained in part from those earnings. When those earnings cease, there must be subsistence both for the dependent boy or girl and for the adult. (Beveridge 1942, Section 402, p 151)

The state and family (inter)dependence

- family = all co-resident family members across three generations (household means test of the 1930s);
- family = co-resident parents and dependent (that is, below school leaving age) children (Public Assistance after 1941 and some postwar means-tested benefits);
- family = parents and dependent children but non-dependants are taken into account in part or distinguished from other adults (some postwar means-tested benefits and Beveridge's plans for National Insurance);
- family = parents including non-resident parents and dependent children (Child Support).

The state intervenes: wartime activity and planning for a new world

The outbreak of war in 1939 had been preceded by plans for the evacuation of children from major urban centres in the likelihood of that eventuality. The expectation of the need to evacuate children as well as infants with their mothers and pregnant women can be seen as a concern with the future of the nation and the need to protect the next generation's adults. However, the impact of the evacuation was to make a much larger proportion of the population sensible of the poverty and deprivation in which many urban children were growing up and to contribute towards a consensus that the state should intervene to prevent such poverty. Initially, the contact between children and householders from widely different walks of life resulted in some shock and complaints from many hosts about the physical, behavioural (and, implicitly, moral) state of their charges. As Padley and Cole, writing as the initial phase of the evacuation unfolded, put it, the "realisation of the immense differences between different social strata" resulted, in the House of Commons debate that took place shortly after the September evacuation had been undertaken, in "the public expression of emotions usually decently concealed. Enuresis and lousy heads were the main topics of discussion. Unfortunately the result was to see in these the results of original sin rather than of social conditions" (Padley and Cole, 1940, p 59). They extend their discussion of this issue when talking of the reactions of hosts themselves:

> What the evacuation scheme did was to make the countryside and the comfortable classes suddenly and painfully aware, in their own persons, of the deep and shameful poverty which exists to-day in the rich cities of England. Dirt and lack of clothing are obviously due principally to poverty; but many people did not realise, though most social workers, even most local government offices in large towns could have informed them, that 'delinquency', in the form of lying, petty thieving and more unattractive vices, is very largely correlated with family income. How should a child be expected to 'respect property', e.g. other children's books and toys, if he has never owned any?... The hosts ... knew as little of the life of the submerged part of the nation as ever did Disraeli's contemporaries; and they felt that they were being swamped by a barbarian invasion. In cold fact, the percentage of children who might be expected to be verminous (which is a fair indication of poverty) ... [gives] 340,000 children in the big cities living in deep poverty; a number sufficiently shocking, one would have hoped, to rouse public opinion to do something about it directly,

rather than write to the papers about the bad language used by their particular evacuee, or his lack of underclothing. (Padley and Cole, 1940, p 73)

Despite the distress caused for many children (as well as their hosts!) by the experience of evacuation, it, and the experience of the war more widely, did nevertheless create an environment in which the valuation of children as investments for the future, and the poverty of children as demanding attention, became core concerns. Moreover, with the experience of increasing state control of living standards through rationing and taxation-funded expenditure, the necessity of avoiding a return to the conditions of the 1930s in the postwar era was also strongly felt.

During the Second World War, then, long-term solutions were sought to avoid a repetition of the experience of the 1930s. Beveridge was invited to look into the issue of *Social insurance and allied services* (Beveridge, 1942). The problem for him was to create a system of insurance entitlements that did *not* allow for dependants alongside a residual assistance system which *did* allow for dependants but was still less generous than insurance. His ideas on entitlement and rates, as well as the anticipated effects of his programme, were derived from the survey research evidence; and he was critically influenced by Rowntree's work in particular. His thinking was more in line with the traditional, family wage-based perspective on families' and children's welfare than on the more radical and feminist perspective from which the family endowment movement (to be discussed later) drew its support. From Beveridge's perspective, the parallel system of insurance and assistance with differentiated rates accorded with principles of justice, thrift, less eligibility and dignity, as well as solving the problem of poverty. Ultimately, however, as he recognised, it could only be ensured by a system of family allowances that would be payable to all but which would be deductible from any social assistance payments. Thus, his proposals included an assumption of family allowances that may have owed much in their substance to the proposals of the family endowment movement and their marshalling of evidence on the welfare – or lack of it – among families; but his motivation for these proposals demonstrated a slightly different logic from that expressed within the movement itself. As the campaign for family endowment (that is, payments to families in relation to the number of children in the family) had pointed out, it offered a potentially more cost-effective policy than a family wage, with no need for intervention in the market or for differential wages between men and women. A form of family allowance had been paid to the families of soldiers serving in the First World War, and this demonstrated the potential for such a scheme to many who might not have countenanced it previously.

The interests of the campaigners for family endowment, however, allied the movement not just with those concerned for child poverty but also with a range of 'women's issues'. These included the recognition of married women's work in the household, the distribution of income within the household and the disparity between men's and women's wages. As Pedersen (1993) has pointed out, the movement was therefore subject to suspicion and this substantially retarded its enactment. Taking her position to its extreme, the research and campaigning around family allowances can almost be seen as having been detrimental to the swifter introduction of allowances.

Eleanor Rathbone is the name most closely associated with this movement (Pedersen, 2004). She campaigned untiringly on this issue up until 1945, when she ensured that payments finally made under the Family Allowances Act of that year were made to the mother rather than to the father. In a lecture in 1927, Rathbone set out many of the arguments in favour of family endowment, also demonstrating how many countries had already put some sort of system into existence. As well as marshalling numerous facts and figures that were increasingly available on the issues of child nutrition and child poverty, she also organised her argument to take issue with countervailing views, in particular the idea that the state should not interfere with parental responsibility:

> The argument that the State must not step in between parent and child has in fact been used against every past measure for safeguarding the welfare of children. Yet few will deny that the standard of parental care has never been higher than at present, and that it has been strengthened by the long series of reforms which have compelled even the most selfish parent to recognize that his child is not merely his creature, but a human being with its own rights and its own value to the community. (Rathbone, 1927, pp 50-1)

But despite her abandonment of the principle of a 'mother's' wage and the fact that she placed her primary arguments around the welfare of children, Rathbone could not but reveal that the family endowment agenda was also driven by concerns with paid and unpaid women's positions. She suggested that acknowledgement of the work done by mothers in bringing up children could be better recognised through 'family endowment' than through the pay packet. Her arguments in relation to the balance of power within the family if the support for children was achieved through a family wage resonate with much more recent debates. They were repeated in discussions on the form in which Child Benefit was to be paid, when family allowances were transformed into this new benefit in 1978, and again with the introduction of Child Tax Credit in 2003, her insights have also found contemporary resonances in the arguments that have made parallels between the role of the paterfamilias and that of the state in relation to women with family responsibilities (Wilson, 1977; see also Lewis, 1984). Rathbone speaks of the emphasis on the "family wage" as disposing

> the father of a family, even while suffering from the failure of wages to meet its ever-changing needs, to look tolerantly on a system which not only makes his wife and children literally his dependants or hangers-on, without a foothold of their own on the economic service of the world, but actually fuses their personalities (economically speaking) with his, so that he acquires a kind of quintuple or multiple personality. It is not suggested that the root-motives of this complex are entirely base or ridiculous. If a man likes the power over his family which the present system gives him, it is not usually (though it may be in a small minority of cases) because he wishes to oppress them. Much oftener probably it is because he craves, in this one relation of an otherwise perhaps obscure and non-potent existence, to feel himself a protector of the weak and a dispenser of good things to the needy. The instinct of chivalry or benevolence, like an intellectual aptitude, desires an opportunity on which to exercise itself. But care is necessary lest the seeming beneficiaries become its victims. (Rathbone, 1927, pp 56-7)

This quotation is interesting because it highlights the complementarity between benevolence and violence within the family that can be seen as paralleled within the state's caring and coercive aspects in relation to families and their needs and responsibilities. The dangers of paternalism within the family are similar to those of state paternalism in relation to the family – although the psychological motives will not be paralleled in the same way.

The contention made so strongly within the family endowment movement that: who controls the resources can be as significant as the total of those resources, has been repeated in more recent arguments, that basing measures of poverty (or lack of poverty) on household income assumes that such income is evenly distributed among the members of a household. For example, Glendinning and Millar (1992, p 9) pointed out that "treating the family as a single unit clearly does not reflect the reality of the way resources are actually distributed within families" (see also Findlay and Wright 1996). Poverty measures applied to families thus, it is argued, tend to overestimate the incomes of women, and correspondingly underestimate the incomes of men, where cohabitation occurs. The actual level of transfers to children and whether they derive equally from both parents' incomes is similarly open to question, but research would suggest that child welfare is better ensured by control through the mother's 'purse' than through the father's 'wallet' (or pay packet) (Good et al, 1998).

Rathbone also noted the extent to which the notion of a breadwinner wage to support the family (such as was supported by Rowntree) was used to justify differential wages to men and women engaged on the same or similar work:

> Nor does it seem probable that, even when trade has become prosperous again, anything less than another Great War will break down the opposition of men trade unionists to the free competition of women's labour with men's, so long as men's wages have to bear nearly the whole burden of the maintenance of the children. This almost inevitably results in different rates of pay for the two sexes, even when the value of their work is admitted to be equal. Or if equal pay is theoretically conceded, it is accompanied by a steady pressure to limit the opportunities of the women workers to the lowest-paid jobs. (Rathbone, 1927, p 35)

However, as mentioned, arguments concerned with the differences between women's and men's pay commanded little political attention, even when allied to family (and child) poverty. Married women were regarded as dependants first, regardless of their actual employment situation, and as workers second. Thus trades unions were more concerned with protecting the value of male wages from undercutting by women than in supporting equal wages. The traditional response to married women's work was only enhanced by policy in 1931, when married women lost entitlement to Unemployment Benefit "unless they could show a 'reasonable expectation' of obtaining insurable work, and that their chances were not impaired by the fact of marriage" (Burnett, 1994, p 206).

The family endowment movement also tried to capitalise on concerns over the declining population to emphasise both the importance of investment in children already alive (the quality issue) and, by implication, the potential impact that such allowances would have on fertility decisions (the quantity issue). As Titmuss and Titmuss (1942) argued, the ideology of capitalism, or 'the assumption of scarcity' (Illich, 1982), rendered beliefs about incentives hard to avoid. (Although the Titmusses argued that such beliefs were misleading and that the concern of social policy with investing in children was valid, whereas attempting to influence fertility behaviour was not an appropriate use of social policy.) The attempt to marshal concerns about fertility in order to justify the introduction of family allowances was in fact unsuccessful, despite the extent of such anxiety (Macnicol, 1980). Social policy in Britain resisted being explicitly pro-natalist, unlike that in France (Gauthier, 1996; Pedersen 1993). This was partly due to political and pragmatic reasons (Titmuss and Titmuss, 1942). It was also logically consistent with concern about introducing incentives of any kind and affecting the responsibility accorded to the working-class family even if there were benefits in national terms to be reaped.

If neither the welfare of families nor population concerns were sufficient to bring into being a system of family allowances, we must look for their inauguration in a combination of the public support mobilised by the Beveridge Report for an overhaul of systems of relief; the fact that Beveridge's proposals needed a system of family allowances to make sense and in the resistance to trades union pressure for wage increases that were felt to be uncompetitive. In the attempt to render the findings of his report politically powerful and to mobilise public opinion behind them, Beveridge orchestrated a highly publicised release of his report. In the days following its publication, 635,000 copies were sold at a price of two shillings each. Mass Observation noted the excitement and the queues that stretched through the streets of London of those trying to get hold of a copy. Beveridge's support for family allowances thus received public endorsement, as well as backing from influential analysts and researchers such as Richard Titmuss and J.M. Keynes. The value of allowances was even recognised by Conservatives due to their potential to keep down wages. In this way, the 1945 Family Allowances Act became inevitable. It established unequivocally the state's acknowledgement of some responsibility for the welfare and costs of children.

For Beveridge himself, this represented an essential shift in position:

> The failure in spite of so much general progress to abolish poverty has been due not simply to lack of knowledge but also to undue emphasis upon a simple line of progress namely improvement of wages and working conditions as distinct from living conditions. Health insurance itself for thirty years has remained, on the side of treatment, confined to the paid workers in place of embracing all the unpaid working population of housewives and dependants.... For improvement of the conditions of people it is more important now to concentrate on living conditions than on working conditions; it is necessary to look away from the workman and his wages at the purpose for which these

> wages are required. To do so, is to see at once that one indispensable
> step to abolition of poverty is the adjustment of incomes to needs by
> children's allowances. (quoted in Fraser, 1984, pp 289-90)

However, as this account has shown, the drive to family allowances also came from far more conservative and pragmatic pressures. Until the final publication of the Act, there also remained concerns that the government would be committing itself and its followers to the substantial maintenance of children and consequently to a great burden. This concern was resolved by removing provision for the first or only child from the scheme and thereby halving the cost. There was also a refusal to set the allowances at a level that reflected contemporary evidence about children's subsistence needs. This meant that there was no implication that the government was committed to taking on the full basic costs of children. We can see here, therefore, an acknowledgement that the state had an obligation to respond to the welfare of children; but that its generosity could always be restricted on economic grounds.

Acceptance of the duty to support children – universally – within the family was not the end of the story. Indeed, as this account has shown, the very introduction of family allowances was built on concerns about producing perverse incentives through funding those out of work too generously, or damaging competition and increasing inflation through pushing up wages of those in work. In the next chapter I look at this crucial issue of the tension between support for children in poverty and concerns with continuing to make work pay as it continued after 1945, particularly in the area of allowances within means-tested support for children. Such concerns continued to be bound up with anxieties about the types of household that were in poverty. On the one hand, anxiety for children was heightened as poverty continued to be seen as a moral failing as well as a state of insufficient income. Moreover, the upbringing of poor children remained a source of concern, and the concept of children as the future nation remained critical, if expressed somewhat differently. On the other hand, the reluctance to consider expensive increases in benefits or to threaten the less eligible status of unemployment compared to employment led to failures to acknowledge continuing child poverty and to insufficiency of allowances – particularly where the wage stop was in operation. Continuing concerns about the health of the economy and the cost of social security also had implications in the failure to increase or even maintain the value of universal support (as can be seen in the future story of family allowances) – or sometimes even its very existence (as illustrated in the history of universal, school-based support).

Notes

[1] Rowntree does not directly describe the qualifications of those used to help with the investigation of heights and weights of the schoolchildren. Instead he states that as the children "came up to be weighted and measured they were classified under the four headings 'Very good', 'Good', 'Fair', or 'Bad', by an investigator whose training and previous experience in similar work enabled her to make a reliable, even if rough, classification" (Rowntree, 1902, p 213).

[2] Rowntree also used the insights of his methodology to argue for a minimum wage (Rowntree, 1918, 1937).

[3] Even the eventual enactment of equal opportunities legislation with the 1970 Equal Pay Act and the 1975 Sex Discrimination Act (both of which came into force in 1975) has been argued as being more part of Britain's preparation to entering the European Economic Community than reflecting concerns with equality.

[4] See Skocpol (1992) on the relationship between military concerns and the rise of the welfare state (in the US).

SIX

Rediscovering child poverty: child poverty and policy from 1945

By the beginning of the postwar period there appeared to be state commitment to a role in supporting children and families with children. However, the measures that had achieved this had not been unequivocal. Moreover, the postwar welfare state began to come under pressure relatively soon and one of the casualties of this was the commitment to children. This chapter explores the revelation that poverty, even child poverty, was not solved, and the subsequent attempts to communicate that fact. This involved both campaigns for increases in support and ongoing attempts to define more precisely the extent of poverty, and to render it conceptually meaningful to policy makers and the public alike.

Transformed lives?

The beginning of the postwar period may have been marked by continued food rationing and an acute housing shortage, but it was also the start of an era in which all families with two or more children received a benefit recognising some of the costs of bringing up children, in which all state schooling was guaranteed to be free up to the age of 15, and in which many other services were also provided within schools to all pupils, either freely, such as the school medical service and milk, or not, such as school meals (although these were free to those in low-income families). Moreover, the 1940s also saw the introduction of a National Health Service in 1948, following the Act of 1946. This opened up possibilities of healthcare to both women and children that had previously been inaccessible due to the limitations of the insurance system. Maternal and child health improved substantially and particular provision in relation, for example, to spectacles and aids for those with hearing impairments now became possible for many families, transforming lives.

Children, whose importance as the future of the nation had been stressed in the plans for evacuation and whose sometimes shocking poverty had been revealed by the carrying out of the programme, seemed to have been confirmed as a core concern of the state. The promises of the 1924 League of Nations Declaration seemed to be being realised, with cross-party support for this position. Titmuss has described the way war can lead to major developments in social policy (Titmuss, 1958): the impact of the Boer war on the liberal reforms of the early years of the 20th century has been noted, as has the role of the First World War in developing systems of family support, which can be seen as being further developed in the provisions for dependants in the 1921 Unemployed Workers' Dependants Act. The 1925 Old Age and Widows and Orphans Contributory Pensions Act, while primarily concerned with supplementing existing old-age provisions available to those aged 70 and over on a means-tested basis, to those aged 65 and over on a contributions basis, also incorporated provisions for the widows and orphans of insured workers. The funding of the Act was to be found through the anticipated decline in the cost of war pensions. These provisions were extended in 1929, and by 1933, 340,000 orphans and their mothers, traditionally two of the poorest and most vulnerable groups, were receiving support through these pensions (Thane, 1996, pp 186-7). The contributory basis kept them away from the Poor Law.

If the First World War was to prompt some advances in social policy, the developments that can be seen to have been produced by the Second World War are, in Titmuss's view, of the same nature, but nevertheless stand out as being more far-reaching:

> In no particular sphere of need is the imprint of war on social policy more vividly illustrated than in respect to *dependant* needs – the needs of wives, children and other relatives for income-maintenance allowances when husbands and fathers are serving in the Forces. To trace in detail the system of Service pay and allowances from the Napoleonic Wars to the Second World War is to see how, as war has followed war in an ascending order of intensity, so have the dependant needs of wives and children been increasingly recognized. The more, in fact, that the waging of war has come to require a total effort by the nation, the more have the dependant needs of the family been recognized and accepted as a social responsibility.
>
> This trend in the war-time recognition of family dependencies has also profoundly influenced social security policies in general. New systems of Service Pay and allowances threw into sharper prominence the fact that in industrial society money rewards take no account of family responsibilities. Nor, until 1939, did many of the payments made under various social services. Thus, one immediate effect was that dependants' allowances were added to Workmen's Compensation and other schemes. Another was that in many respects war pensions and industrial injury pensions had to be brought into line. This was

> done – as so many other things were done – because it seemed
> inappropriate to make distinctions between war and peace, civilians
> and non-civilians. (Titmuss, 1958, p 85)

By the end of the 1940s, then, there was a widespread recognition that
children were a valuable part of society with particular needs that society
as well as the parents had a responsibility to meet. There was a recognition
that children between the ages of 5 and 15 merited free and compulsory
education to suit their abilities; that all children deserved healthcare that
was free at the point of delivery; and that the state had some responsibility
towards sharing the additional costs of children. Rowntree's third poverty
survey suggested that there had been a massive reduction in poverty,
from 31.1% to 2.77% of the working-class population of York living in
the poverty 'classes' A and B (Rowntree and Lavers, 1951). Although
they do not give the proportion of children estimated as being in poverty,
the authors do suggest that large families were the primary cause of
poverty for only 3% of poor families, while old age was the cause in the
case of over two thirds of families (Rowntree and Lavers, 1951, pp 30-
34). While they make some qualifications about their estimates (including
noting that National Insurance rates were insufficient to keep families
above even their 'stringent' poverty line), the picture seemed to be clear,
particularly when reinforced by their findings on the improved heights
and weights of schoolchildren.

The sense that children were of central concern was clearly felt by the
beneficiaries of the new welfare state, as Caroline Steedman's comment
about growing up in the 1950s shows:

> The 1950s was a period when state intervention in childhood was
> highly visible. The calculated, dictated fairness that the ration book
> represented went on into the new decade, and when we moved from
> Hammersmith to Streatham Hill in 1951 there were medicine bottles
> of orange juice and jars of Virol to pick up from the baby clinic for
> my sister. This overt intervention in our lives was experienced by me
> as entirely beneficent, so I find it difficult to match an analysis of the
> welfare policies of the late forties which calls 'the post-war Labour
> government ... the last and most glorious flowering of late Victorian
> philanthropy', which I know to be correct, with the sense of self that
> those policies imparted. If it had been only philanthropy, would it
> have felt like it did? I think I would be a very different person now if
> the orange juice and milk and dinners at school hadn't told me, in a
> covert way, that I had a right to exist, was worth something. (quoted
> in Vincent, 1991, p 150)

However, the motivation for some of the developments was more complex than simply the demands of child welfare, as was shown in the discussion of family allowances. In addition, the levels of consensus would themselves begin to show cracks fairly swiftly. We can note, for example, the resignation of the architect of the NHS, Aneurin Bevin, in 1950 when Gaitskell introduced prescription charges to the 'free at the point of delivery' health service. And the extent to which child poverty had truly been eliminated would itself come into question.

Moreover, analysis would subsequently show that the greatest beneficiaries of the welfare state had in fact been the middle classes. As Brown et al put it:

> If the industrial working class was the driving force behind social change in the nineteenth and early decades of the twentieth century, it is the middle class who are now seen to determine the destiny of post-industrial societies. During the period of economic nationalism [1945-72] the burgeoning middle class benefited most from the expansion of the welfare state, employment security, and the opportunities afforded by comprehensive education and the expansion of post-compulsory provision. (Brown et al, 1997, quoted in Baldock et al, 2003, p 371)

For, underlying the development of a universal valorisation of children and childhood, a number of issues persisted: concerns with keeping out-of-work benefits below the levels of earnings kept allowances for children within means-tested benefits extremely low, while the wage stop continued to ensure that the circumstances of low-paid families remained 'less eligible' out of work than in. Population concerns relaxed somewhat with the 'baby boom' of the 1950s, but investment in quality still remained a key issue. Such investment tended to favour better-off families either indirectly, for example through support for university education, or directly, through child tax allowances that necessarily were more valuable to the better off. Thus nation building, through state intervention with children and families, continued to value the children from middle-class families more, even if eugenicist approaches had ceased to be openly endorsed or expressed. Moreover, unions and traditional forces within governments combined to prioritise tax allowances and reductions that would be felt directly through (largely men's) pay packets over benefits funded by taxation, paid directly to families with children, often to mothers. This chapter highlights these continuities as it discusses the interplay between child poverty research and developments and changes in state support for children. Within research and analysis, we can identify further continuities: on the one hand, close critical attention was paid to the rates and changes in benefits, accompanied by proposals for increases and alterations; on the other hand, there were new approaches being brought to the definition of poverty and to quantifying both the extent of poverty and what that implied for those suffering it.

Making allowances for better-off children

The justification for child tax allowances had come into question in discussion of family allowances in the pre-war period and during the First World War itself. Child tax rebates were first introduced for lower-income tax payers in 1909. They were gradually expanded until by 1920 they covered all tax payers. However, even from their introduction it was primarily middle-class families who benefited from these tax rebates, as working-class families were rarely in the income tax bracket at all at that point. They were therefore regarded by those concerned with child poverty as an inefficient and inequitable way of targeting state support on poor children. At various points it was suggested that the income lost through tax rebates could fund family allowances instead; and in 1939, at a time when the introduction of family allowances was being debated, the value of child tax rebates was one-and-a-half times the cost of the family allowances when they were introduced at the end of the war (Macnicol 1980). Nevertheless, child tax rebates were not used to finance the allowances, as was proposed; instead family allowances were only introduced for the second and subsequent children in order to make the allowance scheme more affordable.

The continuation of tax allowances in the post-1945 era can be seen as a victory for those committed to maximising incentives for child-bearing within the middle class and a partial achievement for those seeking support for families to operate through men's pay packets rather than family allowances paid to women. While it was claimed that the retention of child tax allowances was in order to retain the cooperation of the middle classes in the creation and maintenance of the welfare state, it has also been argued that despite the reluctance to use family allowances to encourage an increase in the birth rate, the interwar government was averse to taking any measures that might contribute to any further lowering of the birth rate among the middle classes. Given the strength of the eugenics movement in the 1930s and the concern with the quality as well as the quantity of the nation's children, it is possible to discern here the obverse to the anxiety about producing perverse incentives among the working class: the fear that middle-class parents would be discouraged from producing children, with a consequent reduction in the numbers of 'higher-quality' children. While eugenics had been discredited since the war and the policies pursued in Nazi Germany, the issue of the 'quality' of the nation's children remained and re-emerged in other forms. Most notably, the rise of the concept of cycles of deprivation in the 1960s problematised children from disadvantaged backgrounds and reasserted an anxiety about the transmission of 'undesirable' characteristics across the generations[1].

Moreover, politicians were also reluctant to support a large-scale shift of resources from the father to the mother, even if the interests of child welfare would be better served by such a shift. Thus, even though campaigners had successfully ensured that family allowances were directly paid to the mother, they were, in many cases, the less valuable element of state support for children. These concerns for measures that supported traditional class and gender hierarchies, even if they were apparently less logical in terms of effective support for children, continued to exert influence at policy level well into the postwar period – despite the attention given to fertility issues with the publication of the report of the Royal Commission on population in 1949.

Researchers had not been slow, in the face of not only the retention but also the expansion of tax allowances in ways that relatively favoured the middle classes, to point out their implications. So unawareness of the impact of tax allowances relative to family allowances could not explain these developments. The extent to which child tax allowances provided a means of direct support to families with children – but support which was greater for those higher up the income scale – had been illustrated (Carr-Saunders et al, 1958; Titmuss, 1958). Titmuss, in his argument for considering fiscal policies alongside explicit social security benefits as part of social provision and spending, described how tax allowances had gradually lost any progressive qualities as they were extended, even as they cost the treasury £200 million in 1955-56, amounting to nearly twice the cost of family allowances. He illustrated his argument

> by considering the respective awards of two married men, one earning £2,000 a year and one earning £400 a year. Both have two children aged under fifteen. The first father now receives an annual net bounty of £97; the second one of £28. [The net bounty is in comparison with a married man without children on the same income, taking account of taxes and allowances and family allowances.] Over the lives of the two families the former will receive a total of £1,455 and the latter a total of £422. (Titmuss, 1958, p 47)

And while Carr-Saunders et al were apparently unconcerned by the regressive implications of their findings, stressing instead that gains as a proportion of earnings are comparable across different earnings levels (resulting in very different absolute gains), they nevertheless provide a similar account of tax allowances combined with family allowances being part of the distribution of state support to children. After giving calculations of the distributions of family sizes, which make it clear that over 40% of children in 1956 were not eligible for family allowances due to being first or only children (and family allowances were payable only to second and subsequent children only up to the introduction of Child Benefit in 1977/78), they go on to point out that:

> ... tax allowances, which in 1957-8 amount to £100-£150 per child (depending on age), are kept distinct from family allowances in official discussions and statistics, largely because their machinery and immediate source of finance differs, but in fact they serve precisely the same end as family allowances. (Carr-Saunders et al, 1958, p 189)

Nevertheless, despite the recognition that tax allowances were an aspect of support to families with children, but one which increased with parents' income, the political will to transfer funding from the regressive tax allowances to the universal system of family allowances was not there. The Labour government from 1964 resisted funding increases in family allowances from child tax allowances; and in its subsequent period of office from 1974, despite a manifesto commitment, it again tried to abandon a scheme to transfer support for families from tax allowances to family allowances that would also cover the first child, after passing the Child Benefit Act that would achieve this in 1975. In this indeterminacy the role of the unions was important, in that they tended to object to the financing of Child Benefit in such a way as would result in a loss of take-home pay, even if there was a net gain in total income. As McCarthy has charted, it was only when the unions were mobilised in support of the new scheme that it was revived sufficiently to be implemented incrementally over the period 1977-78. The extended life of tax allowances can thus be seen as reflecting a resistance to valuing poor children to the same extent as better-off children and a refusal to accept the findings of research and analysis that had clearly shown that family allowances provided an effective and appropriate way to mitigate child poverty.

The tax system was reintroduced as an agent of child support, first with the transformation of Family Credit into the Working Families' Tax Credit, delivered through the pay packet, and subsequently with the Child Tax Credit and the Worker's Tax Credit. However, in these cases, the tax credits take the form of negative income taxes; they are therefore progressive rather than regressive: or in another form they are simply an extension of previous means-tested benefits, but reaching further up the income scale.

One of the key campaigning organisations promoting the translation of child tax allowances into increased and more generous family allowances – or Child Benefit – was the Child Poverty Action Group (CPAG). This organisation had come into being in 1965 in response to the 'rediscovery of poverty' in which many of its founder members had a key role. It was also formed in the context of concerns about 'problem families' and the desire to prevent the transmission of such 'problems' across generations. It was thus an expression of the commitment of those researching poverty and analysing its consequences and effects to achieve change through a lobbying organisation. Such a commitment expressed both the extent of concern at the levels of poverty being endured as well as at inequities within the system and a frustration that the results of research seemed to create no changes in policy. Such frustrations would continue to be expressed in the approach of the CPAG at various points. What, then, had the rediscovery of poverty shown that resulted in the formation of such a group?

Revealing gaps in the welfare state

While there might have been a cumulative endorsement of the achievements of the welfare state, claims that it had eliminated poverty could be regarded as weak in three areas, areas which were gradually taken up and explored systematically. First, the welfare state contained no minimum wage. Low wages would continue to lead to poverty for larger families, particularly if there was only one earner. This was exacerbated by the structure of the family allowance system. The allowances were only payable for second and subsequent children. Moreover, they were set below any recognised levels of subsistence to avoid expectations that the state was taking on responsibility for provision for children, and there was no commitment to uprating them. Indeed, before the introduction of Child Benefit, allowances were only uprated intermittently (for example, after an increase in 1968 they were again kept at a fixed value until 1974), with a consequent decline in their value to families and the further limitation of their possibilities for bringing low-wage families up to a subsistence standard of living. In addition, levels of wages could also affect the incomes of families with an unemployed head, through the operation of the 'wage stop', which kept payments of National Assistance (later Supplementary Benefit) below those which would have been paid in work. If National Assistance rates had represented subsistence levels or a minimum income, then this alone would have forced families below subsistence levels. However, the rates of National Assistance had themselves been set in such a way that they could not be considered to be based on a genuine measurement of minimum needs. Failure to acknowledge, in policy terms, these problems facing the system of state alleviation of poverty meant that poverty persisted. In due course, investigation was carried out by researchers into the adequacy of benefits; and there was ongoing concern with anomalies and inadequacies in the system, as the discussion of tax relief showed. But the 'rediscovery of poverty' was a demonstration that a substantial proportion of the population was living below even the state-sanctioned minimum level of income. It also highlighted the fact that poverty continued to be an issue for the young as well as the old.

The 'rediscovery of poverty' referred to a range of research carried out by a number of academics, largely at the London School of Economics and Political Science, concerned that, in the context of general rising prosperity, a section of the population remained deprived and increasingly divorced from average living standards (Coates and Silburn, 1970). Rowntree and Lavers' (1951) optimistic conclusions had already been questioned in terms of the methodology used to arrive at them in a Political and Economic Planning (PEP) report of 1952[2]. Following this, Peter Townsend's (1957) work on the experience of older people, Dorothy Wedderburn's (1962) and Townsend's (1962) analyses of receipt of National Assistance, the policy analysis of Tony Lynes' (1962) investigation of *Income distribution and social change*, formed systematic contributions to the 'rediscovery', which simultaneously tried to reconceptualise poverty in terms of relating it to wider experiences within society, scrutinise the performance of National Assistance in poverty alleviation and the role of the National Assistance Board in particular, and develop practical schemes for improving the welfare of families. This work was perhaps best synthesised in Brian Abel-Smith and Townsend's (1965) work on *The poor and the poorest*.

Using secondary analysis of two years of the Family Expenditure Survey, Abel-Smith and Townsend explicitly addressed two assumptions that

> ... have governed much economic thinking in Britain since the war. The first is that we have 'abolished' poverty. The second is that we are a much more equal society: that the differences between the living standards of rich and poor are much smaller than they used to be. (Abel-Smith and Townsend, 1965, p 9)

Their analysis used a poverty line of 140% of basic National Assistance levels, to take account of the discretionary extra payments and disregards allowed under National Assistance rules. This summarised for them a poverty line that could be seen as expressing the state's own minimum, although they also performed calculations based on 100% of the basic rate. They estimated that 7.5 million people were living below the 140% measure (including 2.25 million children), and 2 million below the 100% line (of whom one third were children), concluding:

> … the evidence of substantial numbers of the population living below national assistance level, and also of substantial numbers seeming to be eligible for national assistance but not receiving it, calls for a radical review of the whole social security scheme. Moreover, the fact that nearly a third of the poor were children suggests the need for a readjustment of priorities in plans for extensions and developments. (Abel-Smith and Townsend, 1965, p 67)

Townsend was to develop a new approach to defining and measuring poverty in his survey of *Poverty in the United Kingdom* (survey conducted 1969, results published 1979). Nevertheless, even in this work he retained an interest in comparing his measure with one based on a proportion of Supplementary Benefit (which had replaced National Assistance in 1966). Townsend used 140% of Supplementary Benefit as one of his poverty measures in *Poverty in the United Kingdom*, and suggested that there was some match between this level and the deprivation measure that he created. Following his work, a government series called Low Income Families was published, which analysed the composition of those living below 140% of the Supplementary Benefit rate. This series was discontinued in 1985, at least partly, it has been argued, for political reasons, when the Department of Health and Social Security transferred its attention to the creation of 'households below average income' statistics (Johnson and Webb, 1989).

Meanwhile, there was some criticism of the ongoing definition of low income based on subsistence scales. While one aspect of the criticism was that this meant that poverty rates were crucially influenced by the generosity or stinginess of national minima – increases in benefit levels would thus lead to increases in poverty, other things being equal – a further criticism was that such an approach tended to endorse the benefit rates as a reasonable approximation to a viable minimum income. Instead, scrutiny showed that assumptions that benefit rates met some scientifically justifiable standard of minimum needs were not supported by the evidence.

The provision of cash support has historically tended, in Atkinson's word, to 'fudge' the issue of whether needs are explicitly being met by the support and if so, how they are calculated (Atkinson, 1995, p 132). In setting out the basis for a comprehensive social insurance system for Britain, Beveridge faced a number of dilemmas in relation to determining the scales for benefit. He did not plan that National Insurance benefit should be paid at subsistence levels, as that diminished incentives for workers to save for themselves. On the other hand, he considered that National Insurance benefits should be higher than residual National Assistance benefits, since the former had been 'earned' through contributions. However, National Assistance was designed for those without other sources of income, and therefore would have to meet all their needs. Beveridge was also constrained by Treasury pressures to contain costs as far as possible. He drew on Rowntree's research in order to establish his levels for National Insurance and National Assistance benefits respectively in the 1946 National Insurance Act and the 1948 National Assistance Act. However, he used Rowntree's illustrative primary poverty level rather than his subsistence-based Human Needs of Labour line, through a merging of the concept of primary poverty with that of subsistence. It was also, according to Glennerster, Rowntree's attributed causes of poverty that led Beveridge to believe that the National Insurance system would eliminate the majority of cases of poverty (Glennerster, 1995). Beveridge's ultimate rates for National Insurance benefits were not only either 'muddled or mendacious' (Veit-Wilson, 1992), but also assumed payment of family allowances at rates that were not subsequently realised (Beveridge, 1942). In addition, the values at which benefits were set were even lower as a result of inflation that was not fully taken account of, once they came into being in 1946 and 1948. The consequence was that child allowances in National Assistance (there were no dependants allowances in National Insurance) continued to be substantially lower than the amount it would require actually to support a child of the relevant age.

National Assistance levels had been set below subsistence levels (by standards prevailing in the 1930s) in an attempt to ensure that they fell below wage rates (Field, 1985; Veit-Wilson, 1992). Nevertheless, it was found that families with children on low earnings could still be better off out of work and on Assistance than in work. The consequence was the extensive operation of the 'wage stop', a limitation to benefits so that they could not exceed the levels of expected earnings in work. The wage stop had been brought in in 1935, but was very much in line with the principles going back to 1834 and the idea of 'less eligibility'. It continued to be used to suppress benefit payments below what even the state considered a national minimum up to its final abolition in 1975, which followed a long campaign by CPAG as well as by trades unions and other organisations concerned about its impact.

The way benefits were treated after 1946/48 has also been scrutinised by researchers: Bradshaw and Lynes (1995) showed that a variety of policies had been used for uprating and that they had been selectively applied to different benefits. They illustrated that uprating decisions affected the value of benefits so that their real value increased and decreased accordingly over time, and their relative value also varied. In 1973 an earnings or prices formula was introduced as the basis for the uprating of pensions and other long-term benefits, so that they would reap the benefit of whichever was the greater of these two increases; but this principle was broken with the 1980 Social Security Act, and it was never applied to the short-term rate of Supplementary Benefit or to insurance benefits deemed to be 'short term'. Thus, the value of Supplementary Benefit increased very little in real terms over the 1970s and continued to be kept back in relation to rises in earnings in the 1980s.

The value of National Assistance/Supplementary Benefit/Income Support for families of different composition also changed and, as the budget standards approach points out, it tended to undervalue the cost of children. The calculations for relative costs of family members within National Assistance and Supplementary Benefit rates were not based on measured needs so much as assumptions about needs and considerations of worthiness (Piachaud, 1979; Bradshaw, 1993; Parker, 1998) as well as historical precedent (Veit-Wilson, 1992, 1994; Thane 1996). The levels of subsistence benefit as established in the postwar period were crucially influenced by the interaction between work and wages (Macnicol, 1980; Veit-Wilson, 1992) and by concerns in the Treasury about the overall cost, rather than with what was actually necessary to live on; and these concerns continued into the 1990s (Bradshaw and Lynes, 1995, p 29). The change from Supplementary Benefit to Income Support in 1988 brought in a family premium, which gave a boost to the incomes of families with any children. As Adam and Brewer (2004) have pointed out, the trend has been, through such means, for families with one child to benefit proportionally compared to families with several children. This was a shift from the rationale of family allowances, which ignored the first child. The underlying logic for the particular systems of benefit and how they related to needs were not, however, made explicit. A shift in the incomes of families with children on benefit came with the increases in child allowances in Income Support since 2000, such that children now bring in more benefit than the second adult of a couple. The large increase in allowances for younger children (allowances for all children under 16 are now equal) can, however, be related explicitly to research that identified that younger children are no less costly than older ones (Middleton et al, 1997). Increases to both Child Benefit and to the family premium have partly balanced out the relative decline in payments for lone-parent families, which followed the abolition of One-Parent Benefit and the lone-parent premium in Income Support in 1997 – a move that was widely condemned by policy analysts and campaigners (for example, Bradshaw, 2001). The policy logic, was, however, made explicit here – that couple-parent families ('desirable' family forms) should not be penalised relative to lone parents. It was, however, a logic that did not receive much endorsement from researchers, who regarded that the extra difficulties of bringing up children single-handed warranted the additional benefits.

The recognition of the particular circumstances of lone parents dated back to the delayed implementation of Child Benefit in 1975-77, when payments for the first child to lone-parent families preceded the introduction of the full scheme. Nevertheless, benefit rates were insufficient to keep such families out of poverty and the growth of lone-parent families, with their high risks of poverty and benefit receipt has been one of the causes of the increase in child poverty. Lone-parent families create a quandary for governments (Lewis, 2001). They raise the questions of whether the absolute demands of childhood should outweigh concerns over family forms that are not in accord with prevailing ideologies; and whether the single parent (usually mother) should be required to be in employment – taking her away from her traditional caring role. Lone-parent families have become the most recent focus of concern over intergenerational transmission of deprivation and 'the culture of poverty'. Where, at the beginning of the 20th century, large working-class families were seen as aberrant and illustrations of the fecklessness of their parents; towards the end of the century, lone parenthood – and particularly unmarried mothers, although the distinction between forms of lone parenthood is often blurred – have come to be regarded as the problematic family form. At its most extreme, lone parents are implicated in the perpetuation of an underclass (Murray, 1996; see also the discussions in Lister, 1990, and Levitas, 1998); but assumptions about parental responsibility for transmission of problematic values can be found in mainstream policy and in the recent (post-1997) concern with social exclusion (Levitas, 1998).

The provision of additional benefits for lone parents can be seen as a way of acknowledging maternal responsibility; at the same time, the stigmatisation of the benefits received can be seen as reinforcing expectations that couple-parent families are preferable. However, apart from the lone-parent premium incorporated into Income Support on its introduction in 1988, the prevailing attitude has been one of ignoring the issue of the poverty of lone-parent families, despite extensive work emphasising their poverty (Millar, 1989; Rowlingson and McKay, 1998; Lewis, 2001; and see Chapter Two of this book). The engagement with the fact of lone parenthood can be seen to be a shift that took place following the election of the Labour government in 1997. The removal of one-parent benefit/lone-parent premium can be understood as an acknowledgement that lone-parent families were simply another family form, although, as mentioned, the form of action was not one that those wishing for such recognition would have sought. Similarly, the new emphasis on lone parents as potential workers would seem to see them as essentially no different from couple families, where concerns to avoid cycles of disadvantage through transforming non-working families into working families has also been evident. However, this emphasis on the employment of parents could also be argued to be at odds with a focus on the welfare of children themselves, who might be ill-served by the absence of their only parent.

A further way to scrutinise the effectiveness of benefits was to create an external measure against which to evaluate them, effectively returning to the budgetary work of much of the early years of the century. David Piachaud's (1979) study of *The cost of a child* marked a new departure in this respect. Piachaud set out to determine what the minimum costs of a child were and then to evaluate whether the child allowances within Supplementary Benefit matched up to them. Piachaud calculated costs for children aged 2, 5, 8 and 11 (he considered that costing teenagers presented too many problems) and constructed a budget for their maintenance. Taking the bare minimum for food, clothes, additional heat and light, household sundries, presents, pocket money and holidays, school expenses and entertainment, he calculated that Income Support additions for children only made up between 66% and 78% of his budgets, even when take-up of free school meals and milk was assumed.

Following this, the Joseph Rowntree Foundation funded the Family Budget Unit in York in 1985 to investigate and establish an independent measure of what was required for families of different sizes to live at a standard appropriate to social participation. The justification of attempting such a measure of acceptable living standards lay, according to Jonathan Bradshaw, who directed the research, partly in the failure of other research into poverty and living standards to have much effect on the setting of benefit rates, and partly in the need for a measure that would be transparent in its composition and would provide an independent gauge for benefit rates (as well as for other purposes such as assessing fostering allowances and the setting of maintenance orders). As Bradshaw put it in his conclusion:

> Policy makers who have responsibility for making decisions about the level of benefits can be faced through budget standards with the consequence of those decisions. If the low cost budget is more than the income support scales then they can indicate which items in the budget claimants should expect to go without. (Bradshaw, 1993, p 238)

As well as a 'modest but adequate' budget, a 'low cost' budget was also calculated, as were the budget costs of children (Oldfield, 1992, 1993; Oldfield and Yu, 1993; Yu, 1993). From these it could be shown that Income Support rates for couples with two children and a lone parent with two children at 1992 rates made up only 74% and 77% respectively of the low-cost budget standard; while Income Support met only 43% of the costs of a child (after housing costs) and Child Benefit only 17% of the costs of a child according to the 'modest but adequate' standard for children. Further budgets calculated later in the 1990s showed that Income Support levels still compared badly with low-cost budgets for families with children (Parker, 1998); although with more recent increases to Income Support, the gap between the two has narrowed substantially (Bradshaw, 2001).

A feature of research in the postwar period has been, then, to elucidate the failure of benefits, and thus the welfare state, to match up to either practical understandings of minimum needs or their own internal rationales, which has been demonstrated by both the history of family allowances and of National Assistance. The failure of governments to respond to such revelations resulted in the mobilisation of academic researchers concerned with poverty to form a lobbying group. They used an organisation to convey their concerns and proposed solutions directly to policy makers. The 'rediscovery of poverty' in the late 1950s and early 1960s, and the analysis of social security systems, had not received the response among policy makers that had been hoped for. The imperative to action that the continued existence of child poverty presented – and the ways to alleviate it – were clear to these academics, but were not being taken up whole-heartedly within the parliamentary parties. The consequent formation of the CPAG resulted in the creation of a pressure group specifically engaged with securing change in the tax benefit system for the alleviation of child poverty, and one with a core of academics and practitioners who were engaged in trying to set the terms of the debate in relation to the definition and measurement of poverty. The group was to continue as such a campaigning organisation thenceforth. Nevertheless, while it had some access to politicians, particularly Labour politicians, from the start, it could not ensure a positive response to its plans.

Child poverty and family outcomes

From its foundation in 1965, the CPAG campaigned to increase rates of family allowance. The CPAG campaign was partially successful in leading to increases to above 1945 levels in 1968. However, there was frustration at the failure of the Labour government to make further advances in relation to the alleviation of poverty, with the continuation of the wage stop, the reintroduction of prescription charges, also in 1968, and the fact that the increases in family allowances were partially funded by 'clawing them back' through taxation of benefits. The failure to make an impact, despite meetings between CPAG members such as Peter Townsend with ministers in the Labour government in the run-up to the 1970 General Election, resulted in CPAG attempting to make its impact through publicity and media campaigning. The group submitted a statement to the press announcing: "The poor, worse off under Labour – with the Election Campaign about to start, the Child Poverty Action Group has reaffirmed its belief that the poor are worse off as a result of the Labour Government" (McCarthy, 1986, p 130). This was followed by a policy manifesto, *Poor families and the election*, which described how the poor had suffered under Labour in terms of social security. This campaign can be seen as expressing frustration that concerns for welfare of families and the facts about their social security position were not being heard:

> The fact remains ... that the necessity for CPAG to publish *Poverty and the Labour Government* and to conduct a high-profile media campaign in the early weeks of a General Election run-in, only confirms the Group's failure to influence Labour in office and its own exclusion from the official policy community. (McCarthy, 1986, p 136)

If Labour was reluctant to listen, the hoped-for gains from the in-coming Conservative government were also disappointed, when in 1970 the treasury option of a means-tested wage supplement, Family Income Supplement, was introduced in preference to major increases in family allowances and parallel reductions in tax allowances (Glennerster, 1995).

The introduction of Family Income Supplement sparked concerns about both the benefit trap and the appropriateness of subsidising low wages, concerns which did not disappear with the transformation of

Family Income Supplement to the slightly more generous but more time-limited Family Credit[3]. In this context, however, it is interesting to note the parallels between in-work benefits and Abel-Smith and Townsend's earlier argument that a cheaper alternative to increasing family allowances as a partial "remedy for the problem of poverty among children" could be found "by allowing national assistance to be drawn despite the fact that the breadwinner is receiving full-time earnings" (Abel-Smith and Townsend, 1965, p 65): that is, to provide benefits to those in work as well as those out of work up to whatever was deemed to be an appropriate state minimum. The translation of poverty alleviation debated in the research community to policy measures proposed in government will tend to involve both changes in the original idea and in the way it is understood or regarded.

These supplements to working families with children have been a means of acknowledging, again, the unacceptability of child poverty, and the necessity of supplementing the income of poor working families so that their income does not drop below National Assistance/Supplementary Benefit/Income Support levels. Yet by *targeting* child-based benefits on those with low earnings, Family Income Supplement (and its successors) avoided the issue of earnings being insufficient for families with children at one level while creating a higher rank at which families, albeit they were now working, could be better off (or at least as well off) with benefit than when supporting themselves entirely by earnings.

The low-wage supplement to families with children subsequently became transformed into a tax credit – that is, by being offset against tax-deductions – or added on to pay where in excess of tax payable. Proposals for tax credits or 'negative income tax' were first put forward in a 1972 Green Paper from the Conservative government of the day (Vincent, 1991). However, it was under the Labour government of the end of the century that a move towards tax credits began with the metamorphosis of Family Credit to Working Families' Tax Credit in October 1999, and a subsequent split into Child Tax Credit and Working Tax Credit components. The introduction of the minimum wage in advance of the change to the Working Families' Tax Credit partially alleviated concerns about in-work benefits simply subsidising low-paid work, and suggested a more positive approach to redistributing towards families with children. The combination of the minimum wage and Working Families' Tax Credit/Child Tax Credit almost suggested that a compromise had been found to the long-standing dispute over whether low-income families should be supported through the pay packet or through a 'mother's wage', especially given that the Child Tax Credit is paid to the primary carer (usually the mother).

Levels of pay were also significant in relation to the developing consensus that a measure of poverty had to be regarded as a relative rather than an absolute concept. The 'rediscovery of poverty' had drawn attention to the fact that poverty was persisting despite rises in earnings and in average standards of living. Townsend built on this insight in his survey of *Poverty in the United Kingdom,* for which in preference to re-using government data, he designed a particular survey involving a particular method of measuring deprivation. Townsend's measure of poverty examines a series of indicators of 'normal' life and then surveys a sample of the population to determine if there is a level at which deprivation in these areas increases disproportionately with a drop in income. The indicators covered what Townsend considered "the major areas of personal, household and social life" (Townsend, 1979, p 251). Townsend distinguished his method, which he termed the Deprivation Standard of Poverty, from two types of relative poverty: the composition of the bottom 10% of the income bracket, or all those falling below a somewhat arbitrary proportion of average income, say 50%. In fact it is these latter measures which in practice make up most of the poverty statistics available to us now. Townsend determined that in 1969, 23% of the population fell beneath his deprivation standard, while 28% fell beneath the 'state standard' which was based on 140% of Supplementary Benefit rates.

There has been extensive criticism of both Townsend's method and his findings – the most stringent coming perhaps from Piachaud, who commented tartly that: "There can be no doubt that Townsend's provisional deprivation index is of no practical value whatsoever as an index of deprivation" (Piachaud, 1981, p 420), as well as criticising Townsend's claims to objectivity. Nevertheless, conceptually Townsend's work was important in establishing the idea that (in)ability to participate as a citizen should be fundamental to the way poverty was conceived and measured. As he himself asserted:

> Poverty can be defined objectively and applied consistently only in terms of the concept of relative deprivation....The term is understood objectively rather than subjectively. Individuals, families and groups in the population can be said to be in poverty when they lack the resources to obtain the types of diet, participate in the activities and have the living conditions and amenities which are customary or are, at least, widely encouraged or approved, in the societies to which they belong. Their resources are so seriously below those commanded by the average individual or family that they are, in effect, excluded from ordinary living patterns, customs and activities. (Townsend, 1979, p 31)

The insight into the relativity of poverty was in many ways critical and began by and large to become accepted as the only way of measuring poverty and of looking at trends over time. We can note here the EU definition:

> ... the poor shall be taken to mean persons, families and groups of persons whose resources (material, cultural and social) are so limited as to exclude them from the minimum acceptable way of life in the Member State in which they live. (European Commission, 1984, quoted in Gordon et al, 2000, p 12)

Nevertheless, the opposition of absolute and relative measures also became something of a hostage to fortune, both in relation to those who wished to deny the existence of poverty –

> A family is poor if it cannot afford to eat.... By any absolute standards there is very little poverty in Britain today (Lord Joseph, 1976, quoted in Oppenheim and Harker, 1996, p 8)

– and in stimulating a series of academic debates on the definition of poverty that seemed to create a certain distance from the subjects of poverty themselves and from the policy imperative implied by that, as Piachaud (1987) warned. Veit-Wilson (1986a, 1986b) pointed out that in stressing the relative nature of poverty, Townsend was creating an idea of an absolute measure that had never actually been employed; while Sen built on the intuitive understanding of poverty as an absolute lack by distinguishing the absolute nature of capabilities from their relative realisation:

> Some capabilities, such as being well nourished, may have more or less similar demands on commodities (such as food and health services) irrespective of the average opulence of the community in which the person lives. Other capabilities, such as the ones with which Adam Smith was particularly concerned, have commodity demands that vary a good deal with average opulence. To lead a life without shame, to be able to visit and entertain one's friends, to keep track of what is going on and what others are talking about, and so on, requires a more expensive bundle of goods and services in a society that is generally richer, and in which most people have, say, means of transport, affluent clothing, radios or television sets, etc. Thus, some of the same capabilities (relevant for a 'minimum' level of living) require more real income and opulence in the form of commodity possession in a richer society

than in poorer ones. The same absolute levels of capabilities may thus have a greater relative need for incomes (and commodities). There is thus no mystery in the necessity of having a 'relativist' view on the space of incomes even when poverty is defined in terms of the same *absolute* levels of basic capabilities. (Sen, 1987, p 18)

In fact, as Ringen (1988) among others has pointed out, the distinction between relative and absolute is a spurious one. Poverty is necessarily tied to its context and deprivation must exist in relation to cultural context. Nevertheless, the dichotomy is one which continues to command wide currency (for example, Fimister, 2001), something that is reinforced by the use of the notion of relativity in the specific context of the proportions of average earnings that make up the most commonly employed low-income measure in the *Households below average income* series. And indeed it is this series, based initially on the Family Expenditure Survey (the source originally used for Abel-Smith and Townsend's 1965 analysis) and subsequently on the Family Resources Survey, a specially-designed government survey initiated in 1993/94 in order to provide detailed income information for the population based on a large survey, that has continued to reveal excess low income experienced by children relative to the average for the population as a whole, and to provide the headline figures of child poverty that were used to stimulate a consensus that it was a social ill that needed to be tackled by the current Labour administration. Comparable analysis was also used to describe the way that children had fared over an extended period. Gregg et al (1999), using the Family Expenditure Survey, found a rapid increase in the numbers of children living below half average income from 1.3 million in 1968 to 4.3 million in 1995/96, despite the facts that a smaller proportion of families now contain children and that the average size of families had decreased. They also found that over the 16 years from 1979, poverty, measured as 50% of the 1979 average held constant across time, had barely declined, while general living standards had risen by nearly one third. The authors argued that poverty had increased for families with children more and more rapidly, than for other types of family and that thus children had suffered disproportionately.

Reasserting the reality of child poverty

As well as attempting to take Townsend's method one stage further, the impetus towards the Breadline Britain surveys and work on deprivation as a measure of poverty must surely be seen in part as resulting from a concern that the reality of poverty was in danger of being lost behind debates on definition – even though it stimulated further debates – and by the claims that relative poverty was not poverty at all but 'merely' inequality. The Breadline Britain survey attempted to develop a democratic measure of poverty based on 'ordinary people's' perceptions of necessity (Mack and Lansley, 1985). Their study, claimed the authors,

> ... aims to identify a minimum acceptable way of life not by reference to the views of 'experts', nor by reference to observed patterns of expenditure or observed living standards, but by reference to *the views of society as a whole*. This is, in essence, a *consensual* approach to defining minimum standards. (Mack and Lansley, 1985, pp 42-3; original emphasis)

They therefore asked their sample to decide which of 35 items they deemed to be necessities. Those with more than 50% support, they then argued, were consensually approved as necessities of life and should constitute the minimum standard (at that time). They also asked people which of the items they had and which they could not afford. And they asked people whether they would be prepared to pay an extra penny in tax in order that everybody should have these things.

There was extensive criticism of the desirability and practicality of 'consensual' methods of measuring poverty (Piachaud, 1987; Veit-Wilson, 1987; Walker 1987). It was pointed out that consensus is not the same as a majority view; and the rejection of 'expert' opinion also came under attack: it was pointed out that the list of potential necessities was drawn up by the investigators rather than their subjects, who had the rather more passive role of selecting essentials from it. A further problem with the consensual approach is that it does not relate consensus of opinion to consensus of political action, except in the most limited and hypothetical way, by asking respondents if they would be prepared to pay more Income Tax to ensure that people could have those things considered necessities. The value of this debate, I suggest, was that it emphasised the distinctness between poverty and measurement and political action. While political action may require measures of poverty, and measures of poverty conducted in particular ways, the act of measurement can only ever have the requirement for action implicit within it.

Mack and Lansley repeated their survey of 1983 in 1990 (Gordon and Pantazis, 1997). They found that poverty, according to their measure, had increased from 14 to 20%, which parallels the growth in inequality when estimated by a relative income measure over a similar period (Goodman et al, 1997). The approach was also related to that used in the *Poverty and social exclusion in Britain* survey (Gordon et al, 2000). This survey was related to the developments in deprivation indices and the conceptualisation of poverty in terms of 'lacks', which links back to Townsend's work and to attempts to make the definition of poverty more clearly realisable (Nolan and Whelan, 1996). The influence of this way of conceiving of and measuring poverty has been recognised in the importance accorded it in the recent consultation on measuring child poverty (DWP, 2003a).

A further way in which relatively recent research has contributed to understandings of poverty, which is again pursued or justified, in part at least, as a way of making poverty both comprehensible and to convey its reality, is in the development of longitudinal measures. As Walker and Ashworth argued, "without taking time into account it is impossible fully to appreciate the nature and experience of poverty or truly to understand the level of suffering involved" (Walker with Ashworth, 1994, p 1). Rowntree's original insights into the experience of poverty had been as a primarily longitudinal phenomenon, as the following quotations show:

> Many of these [currently in poverty] will, in course of time, pass on into a period of comparative prosperity; this will take place as soon as the children, now dependent, begin to earn. But their places below the poverty line will be taken by others who are at present living in that prosperous period previous to, or shortly after, marriage. Again, many now classed as above the poverty line were below it until the children began to earn. The proportion of the community who at one period or other of their lives suffer from poverty to the point of physical privation is therefore much greater, and the injurious effects of such a condition are much more widespread than would appear from a consideration of the number who can be shown to be below the poverty line at any given moment. (Rowntree, 1902, pp 136-7)

> The fact remains that every labourer who has as many as three children must pass through a time, probably lasting for about ten years, when he will be in a state of 'primary' poverty; in other words, when he and his family will be *underfed*. (Rowntree, 1902, p 135; emphasis in original)

However, Rowntree lacked adequate tools to measure it in this way and so used illustrative devices, such as a graph of the periods of life above and below the poverty line (see Rowntree's timeline of poverty in the box below), and his powers of explication to express it. During the 1930s, the Pilgrim Trust considered the duration of men's unemployment as well as its extent, finding that a substantial proportion of unemployed people had been so for five years or more, and that unemployment of under a year was the experience of only a minority of unemployed people in some areas. The effects on adults of long periods of poverty were described by observers such as George Orwell. However, it was early recognised that the duration of poverty could be particularly significant for children, long periods of poverty having the potential permanently to impair their health and development. The development of both methods and data resources for examining childhood poverty enabled the communication of how child poverty is divided between temporary, permanent and recurrent poverty, with the implications for their contemporary well-being (as children) and for their future potential (as the nation's adults and workers).

For example, Hill and Jenkins (2001) drew attention to the issue of the experience of chronic poverty among young children and the difficulty of targeting it. They also highlighted the marked differences in experiences of poverty among younger and older children. A form of longitudinal measurement of poverty was incorporated into the Opportunity for All targets for children, alongside other measures, thus acknowledging the importance of poverty as a dynamic concept (see also the DWP-commissioned study, Jenkins and Rigg, 2001). Moreover, the relationship between deprivation and income can be better understood when deprivation is considered as a consequence of poverty over time rather than as a possibly short-term occurrence of low income. It transpires, unsurprisingly, that it is the element of time that explains the difference between those suffering deprivation as a result of current low income and those who are not. Studies of child poverty measured longitudinally have also been susceptible to comparative analysis, revealing how well (or poorly) Britain's institutions succeed in preventing long-term as well

Rowntree's timeline of poverty and its relation to the five stages of life

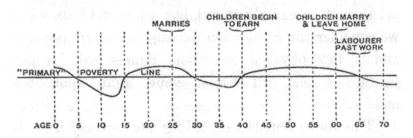

Source: Taken from *Poverty: A study of town life*, B.S. Rowntree (Macmillan, 1902)

as transitory poverty, compared to other nations (Bradbury et al, 2001; Jenkins et al, 2003).

Child poverty in international context

Despite the pressures put on the welfare state in the period 1979-97, the increasing acknowledgement of the unique and uniquely valuable status of the child was reinforced by concern at an international level. Following on from being signatory of the 1924 League of Nations Declaration on the Rights of the Child, Britain subsequently became signatory to the 1959 United Nations Declaration on the Rights of the Child, and, most recently, the 1989 United Nations Convention on the Rights of the Child. While the 1989 Convention was less emphatic than was originally envisaged (Alston, 1994), it nevertheless included provisions relating to the maintenance of children (UN, 1996). In Article 26, it states the right of every child to benefit from social security; and Article 27 states the right for an adequate standard of living for the child, which is to be primarily the responsibility of the parents, with the state's assistance where necessary, and in accordance with 'national conditions' and means. Article 27 also provides for states to recoup such costs from parents where possible. Signatories to the Convention are required to produce regular reports identifying their fulfilment of, or towards, the requirements of the Articles. In the UK's 1999 report, however, Article 26 gained little attention, while Article 27 was commented on by a pointer to the government's consultation document *Supporting families* (Home Office, 1998), which included a proposal to "give better financial support to families to improve family prosperity and reduce child poverty" (DoH, 1999, p 20).

Britain's international obligations relating to poverty

1989 United Nations Convention on the Rights of the Child.
• Periodic reports on fulfilment of the Convention required under Article 44
• Second periodic report 1999 (DoH, 1999)

2000 Lisbon European Council
• European Union commitment to making a decisive impact on the eradication of poverty by 2010
• Bi-annual action plans on social inclusion required
• *National action plan on social inclusion 2003-05* (DWP, 2003b)

The increasing availability of international comparisons combined with interest in harmonisation of data at an international level has made Britain's levels of child poverty visible in comparison with other countries. Thus, for example, the UNICEF 'league tables' highlighted the poor showing of Britain in terms of its ability to relieve child poverty, despite its strong economic position (Bradbury and Jäntti, 1999; see also UNICEF, 2000; Vleminckx and Smeeding, 2001; Micklewright, 2003). Such rankings, whatever their methodological problems, have a transparency that is hard to resist. They are also influential in terms of the constraints upon their measures (that is, their need for similar sources and definitions across all countries to be considered) creating a reference point for refutation or cross-checking of their findings. Moreover, studies such as Bradshaw et al's (1993) work on child support in cross-national perspective have revealed the relative generosity, or lack of support, of different systems of provision for children; while Kamerman et al (2003) have addressed the relationship between policy, family types and child poverty. When repeating the approach of Bradshaw et al (1993) more recently (and with 22 countries), Bradshaw and Finch (2002) were able to show that Britain had substantially improved its ranking in terms of the generosity of its income package for children.

As a member of the European Union, Britain is also affected by the development of a Europe-wide series of indicators for measuring poverty and social exclusion, against which it will be evaluated over time and comparatively with other European Union states (Atkinson et al, 2002). The creation of a group to develop this set of indicators was established in 2000 and the indicators were adopted in 2001 as a step towards making a decisive impact on eradicating poverty within member states by 2010. The indicators are on two main levels – 'lead' indicators and supporting and supplementary indicators. They include measures of financial poverty, income inequality, poverty persistence and joblessness as well as health, housing and education. The indicators cover all individuals (including children) rather than specifying specific targets for child poverty, as the British government did in 1999.

However, a Europe-wide agenda for addressing child poverty has been separately established by EURONET, the European Children's Network, which campaigns for children's rights and for the greater visibility of children within European Union policy and legislation. A report on *Including children?* identifies children as particularly in need of consideration in relation to poverty because of their vulnerability – but also because of the potential damage to the future of member states (Ruxton and Bennett, 2001). Recalling long-standing and recurrent justifications for intervention (or non-intervention) that have been considered in this book, the authors argue that it is essential to "achieve social consensus on core values (for example, about children as a shared responsibility and social investment, rather than as the private property, or the sole responsibility of their parents)" (Ruxton and Bennett, 2001, p 5). However, they also stress the importance of the child's perspective on social exclusion, an aspect which has been predominantly absent in research and campaigning around child poverty in Britain[4].

The international context in which what it means to be a 'civilised' country can be looked for in a nation's treatment of its children offers the possibility, then, for comparative research to challenge a government's record and role with reference to external points of reference. Moreover, issues of national investment and future competitiveness, which mean that states value children not just for themselves but also for their potential as adults, and which stimulated much of the early development of intervention in poor children's lives, become particularly salient at the point of such comparisons.

Notes

[1] In 1972 Keith Joseph highlighted the issue of 'cycles of deprivation', seeing in the concept an explanation for the continuation of child poverty and he launched a major research programme into this area. See Deacon (2002).

[2] The Rowntree and Lavers study itself had surrounded its conclusions with various caveats, which were not often acknowledged in the use made of it to endorse the successes of the welfare state.

[3] Although it is worth noting that the increases in Family Credit compared to Family Income Supplement came at the expense of children's eligibility for free school meals. An amount to cover this loss was notionally included in Family Credit, but obviously would be hard to earmark when family budgets came under pressure. This illustrates part of the move away from 'direct' support that is argued as distinguishing this period.

[4] Although there are obviously a few exceptions, for example, Ridge (2002).

SEVEN

Conclusion:
child poverty on the agenda

Child poverty and its alleviation – or even elimination – has now reached an uncontentious position as a priority for government. It would seem that the facts and impacts of child poverty as demonstrated incrementally through research have been finally accorded unequivocal recognition. To what extent, however, is this a permanent shift in approach? To what extent does it represent a genuine break with past approaches? And to what extent does it represent a direct translation from the demonstrable findings of research to political will and universal consensus? Only time can answer the first question – although history demonstrates that there have been other periods (most notably after the Second World War) where an apparent consensus on the value of children's welfare has been achieved only to be undermined subsequently. Meanwhile, this chapter highlights some remaining issues to consider in relation to child poverty at the end of the 20th century; and it also summarises the problematic relationship between research and policy that has marked the last 200 years and cannot be said to have been resolved in the present day.

In his Toynbee Hall lecture, Tony Blair made it clear that children were a priority, that poor children were a particular source of concern, but that the state also had a commitment to all children:

> Above all our welfare reform programme will give children – all children – the support they need. Our approach on children brings together all the lessons we have learned from applying reform in other areas.... The levels of child deprivation are frightening.... And in the last 20 years the tax burden on families has increased. At the very time that families have come under increasing pressure, juggling work and home, the state has made it harder than ever for them to cope.

> We need to break the cycle of disadvantage so that children born into poverty are not condemned to social exclusion and deprivation. That is why it is so important that we invest in our children.

> But our reforms will help more than the poorest children. All parents
> need help. All children need support.
>
> Across government, children are getting a better deal. Our family
> policy is geared to children and their well-being more than the type
> of family that a child is born to. (Blair, 1999, pp 15-16)

Children, per se, then, and particularly child poverty, had been put high
on the political agenda, and targets were put in place for the stages in
which elimination of child poverty was to be measured and the forms in
which it was going to be assessed.

Analysis by Stuart Adam and Mike Brewer (2004) showed that since
1999, state spending on financial support for children within families or
on support to families that was dependent on them containing children
('child-contingent' support) had increased by 52% in real terms. This was
more than the overall increase across the preceding 25 years. They also
point out that the increase in spending per child since 1999 has been
almost entirely a consequence of policy changes, rather than a result in
changes in the characteristics of households with children, that had driven
some of the preceding increases in expenditure. There has clearly been a
willingness to follow the commitment to children with government
expenditure.

Moreover, the aim seemed to be one which commanded a fair degree
of consensus: the elimination of child poverty was not a topic that could
really invite debate. In his discussion of Blair's Toynbee Hall lecture of 18
March 1999, Robert Walker comments that:

> Blair's new commitment in the Lecture to end child poverty within
> 20 years was met with a considerable degree of accord in both the
> tabloids and the broadsheets. There was discussion about the
> appropriateness of the time-scale and about the absence of a precise
> definition of poverty and, in some quarters, a world-weary scepticism
> about Labour's true intentions, but little direct hostility. (Walker, 1999a,
> p 3)

However, the extent to which this consensus is strong enough to survive
changes in administration or in the economy has been questioned. While
acknowledging that the agenda had been altered 'in a very real way', the
CPAG were still concerned, reflecting that "making sure that this impetus
is maintained is, of course, a major challenge for both the Government
and the poverty lobby – especially if changes of political administration
or in economic circumstances ... intervene" (Fimister, 2001, p 3).

Meanwhile, without changes in the administration, the Chancellor of the Exchequer pursued a review of the extent to which the government was on target to meet its child poverty objectives (halving child poverty by 2010, eliminating it by 2020, and with an interim target of reducing it by a quarter by 2004/05) (HM Treasury, 2004). The review, a commitment of the previous year's Budget (2003), explored, with extensive consultation with academics, campaigning organisations and local authorities, both what progress was being made and what measures were necessary to keep on target with this overall aim and the associated Public Service Agreement targets.

Despite the optimistic tenor of this review, and despite working definitions of child poverty measurement (see, for example, the Department for Work and Pensions' *Opportunity for All* indicators and annual reports and the recent consultation on *Measuring child poverty* [DWP, 2003a]), and despite some substantial increases in the child elements of Income Support and on-going increases in the allowances for children within the tax credit system, there remains no explicit recognition of a government responsibility to maintain at a particular level – or what the basis of such a level might be. There has clearly been a willingness to involve outside comment on the different ways that progress is to be evaluated, and in a search for an 'ultimate' measure of child poverty. However, the catch-all approach allows for a certain degree of blurring of cause and effect in what constitutes child poverty, as well as continuing to obscure the exact nature of the state's role and commitment.

> It is unlikely that a single measure or approach will adequately capture everyone's view of poverty.... Overall there were a wide range of opinions.... This reflects the complexity of the issues involved. What is also apparent from the consultation is that there is no 'perfect' measure and there are problems associated with all of the possible options put forward. (DWP, 2003a, pp 2-3)

There may be a risk, then, that the incorporation of researchers into the process of evaluating government targets may lose, in the refinement of understandings of measurement, any clear notion of what is being measured and why.

Meanwhile, as well as substantial breaks with preceding eras, we can also note a number of continuities. The importance of a healthy economy in maintaining levels of support has been, and will surely continue to be, significant. We can also observe continuation notions of cultural aspects of poverty and the upbringing of children in discussions of cycles of disadvantage and in the definition of and stress on social exclusion

(Deacon, 2002; Welshman, 2002). It is notable that in its first few years, the majority of the reports coming from the Social Exclusion Unit were related to children or young people: those excluded from school, teenage pregnancy, runaways, and so on. This also emphasises the continuing concern with children as an investment, as 'the future'. A further example of this can be found in the following extract from a Department for Employment and Education report, which suggests that poorer children have to justify their investment more than all children:

> All children, especially those who are disadvantaged or deprived, need to be equipped properly for the challenges of the new century, so they can achieve their potential. (DfEE, 2000, p 9)

It is possible to observe in such statements continuing overtones of the tension between childhood as something to be valued in its own right, and children as primarily incipient adults. Moreover, the stress on "those who are disadvantaged or deprived" indicates that this tension is more palpable in relation to children from poor backgrounds. Their construction as children is subservient to their role as workers and citizens of the future. While parents' support for children may have come to be justified in terms of the returns (emotional and otherwise) that they derive from children themselves (Zelizer, 1985), support from the state in lieu of such parental support requires returns in the future.

The establishment of the particular status of childhood and the necessity for child support has, then, been accepted, but also remains contingent. A similar point may be made for the acceptance of the role of research into child poverty in establishing the framework for policy development. If we reflect back on the relationship between research and policy over the last 200 years, one message that comes over from this survey of poverty studies and policy change is that there exists an oblique relationship between the two. Developments in child poverty research, in child welfare policy, and in the conceptual distinction of the child interacted with each other throughout the period under consideration. Direct causal relationships, however, remain hard to disentangle as they could work in both directions. Conclusions about the impact of research on policy must remain, at most, tentative. Nevertheless, it remains undeniable that the world of today is very different from that of 1800. There has been extensive policy development over the period and the development of systematic empirical research was both associated with the policy developments and was increasingly recognised as an important point of reference for future development. This book has attempted to illustrate some of the major developments in, and insights of, child poverty research, and also the extent to which, and the conditions under which, they and associated campaigning activities, were acknowledged at the policy level. Two short examples can be used to summarise some of the problematics of research influence here.

It is undeniable that Rowntree's (1902) *Poverty* study had a significant and far-reaching impact, which can still be felt in today's welfare state. It was not, however, an impact that derived directly from his research and conclusions. Much of Rowntree's development of his insights into poverty revolved around the notion of a minimum or 'breadwinner' wage – yet it was only in 1999, 100 years after his first research in York, that Britain saw the introduction of a minimum wage as part of a concerted anti-poverty policy. Similarly, while much poverty research and lobbying has been motivated by the existence of child poverty, the realisation of adequate child poverty reduction measures has often been at variance with other policy concerns, in particular concerns around perverse incentives – that is, not making unemployment 'attractive' to parents.

Equally, Eleanor Rathbone's name is synonymous with the movement for family allowances. Yet, despite her tireless campaigning from after the First World War, family allowances were only finally introduced in 1945, and even then with some resistance. Their introduction can be seen to have served a number of alternative policy pressures (for example, wage suppression), as well as solving the conundrum of setting both appropriate but distinct National Insurance and National Assistance rates. In fact, the association of the family allowance movement with the feminist movement and with concerns for some financial autonomy for women resulted, as Pedersen argued, in the limited effectiveness of the highly energetic campaign.

A further finding is that to create its impact, research not only had to come of age, but, almost paradoxically, it also had to appeal to conservative instincts in order to effect policy change. This is not to downplay the impact of single-issue and radically-based campaigning. The campaign for protective factory legislation can be seen as a highly radical one that mobilised support through its emotive highlighting of child labour. In fact, it drew little on what we might see as conventional research. Nevertheless, such activism clearly had to locate more traditional power bases of support in philanthropic individuals and organisations and those concerned with church-based education. It also had to accord, at least in part, with wider policy objectives before it could really have effect. Similarly, the campaign to win increases in family allowances in the 1960s and 1970s had to find a way of mobilising union support, initially opposed to the changes, if it was to gain sufficient political influence to have an impact.

The assumed relationship between the welfare of women and of children led to policy initiatives based on these interconnections. The fact that women give birth to, and have tended to be responsible for the care of, children resulted in health and welfare interventions for children being aimed directly at women. At the same time, mistrust of the capability of working-class mothers meant that attention was both paid to their 'education' and to identifying spaces (particularly schools) where interventions could be made more directly. Such policy could be embraced or rejected by feminists and by those primarily concerned with the welfare of children. Policy for children and women has also often been connected by assumptions that they are in an equivalent situation: as dependants or as needing protection. Thus, restrictions on women's employment followed restrictions on child labour. In addition, women's responsibility for children was argued to be both a reason for a family wage rather than wage equality between men and women, and for an allowance paid directly to women to enable them to control the family finances more effectively in favour of children.

One of those critical shifts that was crucial to the implementation of policy in relation to the education and welfare of children, but which was also born of such policy, was the changing status of childhood over the period. Policy change itself fed into an increasing concern with the situation of the child, which then prompted mobilisation of activity around the issue of child welfare, itself resulting in policy changes and shifts. As this book has illustrated, the issue of and response to child poverty cannot be separated from those processes (such as education and labour control) by which the boundaries of childhood became fixed in terms of both age and space. Nevertheless, while this marking out of childhood involves the gradual recognition of children as 'children' first and 'poor' second, such recognition does not result in an unequivocal response to child poverty. The prevailing ideologies of the day, the perception of children as primarily the responsibility of their parents, and the emphasis on engendering a responsible public means that active measures to ameliorate the poverty of children can be resisted. Developments in poverty research, and the consequent developed understanding of children's needs, can stimulate a breakthrough in approaches to child poverty. But it may take additional conditions that shift conventional positions on existing levels of welfare to increase pressure for appropriate responses.

Research has provided the means for pressure groups to pursue their goals and can be seen in the continuing action of, for example, the CPAG or the Save the Children Fund, as well as organisations such as Shelter, which highlight particular aspects of children's deprivation. Yet its impact is not predictable, and research findings do not lead conclusively to action.

Moreover, pressure groups themselves utilise research findings in particular and selective ways to support positions that are themselves contextually specific and need historical exploration – as, for example, the role of such organisations as Barnardo's in child emigration, demonstrate. Not only the solution to child poverty but even what constitutes child welfare will be understood differently at different times. Child poverty research has contributed to both the conceptualisation of the 'problem' and proposals for solutions. The way that both are utilised and interpreted may not, however, be as practitioners imagine or intend; and it will not automatically receive an audience. Rather, research has to find its place within prevailing (although obviously not static) ideas and beliefs. In order to move forward, research has had to juggle between a radical agenda that would mobilise interest and action and more conventional positions, such as on women's claims to equality.

Nevertheless, despite this less than optimistic scenario, the role of both key activists and innovative research has been critical. Poverty researchers can be seen to have developed and defined a field of research, which is a critical element in enabling child poverty as a subject to be talked about and engaged with as a policy issue. Without the work of research to both define the problem and then to reiterate it in up-to-date or modified forms, the policy agenda would not advance.

References

Abel-Smith, B. and Townsend, P. (1965) *The poor and the poorest*, Occasional Papers on Social Administration, 17, London: G. Bell & Sons.

Acheson, D. (Chair) (1998) *Independent inquiry into inequalities in health* (The Acheson Report), London: The Stationery Office.

Adam, S. and Brewer, M. (2004) *Supporting families: The financial costs and benefits of children since 1975*, Bristol: The Policy Press.

Aldgate, J. and Tunstill, J. (1995) *Making sense of section 17: Implementing services for children in need within the 1989 Children Act*, London: HMSO.

Alston, P. (1994) 'The best interests principle: towards a reconciliation of culture and human rights', in P. Alston (ed) *The best interests of the child: Reconciling culture and human rights*, Oxford: Clarendon Press, pp 1-25.

Archard, D. (1993) *Children: Rights and childhood*, London: Routledge.

Ariès, P. (1962) *Centuries of childhood*, trans. R. Baldick, London: Jonathan Cape.

Ashworth, K., Hardman, J., Hartfree, Y., Maguire, S., Middleton, S., Smith, D., Dearden, L., Emmerson, C., Frayne, C. and Meghir, C. (2002) *Education Maintenance Allowance: The first two years: a quantitative evalution*, DfES Research Report 352, London: HMSO.

Ashworth, K., Hardman, J., Liu, W.-C., Maguire, S., Middleton, S., Dearden, L., Emmerson, C., Frayne, C., Goodman, A., Ichmura, H. and Meghir, C. (2001) *Education Maintenance Allowance: The first year,* DfEE Research Brief No. 257, London: DfEE.

Atkinson, A.B. (1995) *Incomes and the welfare state: Essays on Britain and Europe*, Cambridge: Cambridge University Press.

Atkinson, A.B., Cantillon, B., Marlier, E. and Nolan, B. (2002) *Social indicators: The EU and social inclusion*, Oxford: Oxford University Press.

Atkinson, A.B., Corlyon, J., Maynard, A.K., Sutherland, H. and Trinder, C.G. (1981) 'Poverty in York: a re-analysis of Rowntree's 1950 survey', *Bulletin of Economic Research*, vol 33, pp 59-71.

Baldock, J., Manning, N. and Vickerstaff, S. (2003) *Social policy* (2nd edn), Oxford: Oxford University Press.

Banton, M. (1998) *Racial theories*, Cambridge: Cambridge University Press.

Beveridge, W. (1942) *Social insurance and allied services*, Cmd 6404, London: HMSO.

Blair, T. (1999) 'Beveridge revisited: a welfare state for the 21st century', in R. Walker (ed) *Ending child poverty: Popular welfare for the 21st century?*, Bristol: The Policy Press, pp 7-18.

Booth, C. (1903) *The life and labour of the people in London* (17 vols), London: Macmillan.

Bosanquet, H. (1973 [1914]) *Social work in London 1869-1912*, Brighton: The Harvester Press.

Bowley, A.L. (1898) *The statistics of wages in the United Kingdom during the last hundred years*, London: Royal Statistical Society.

Bowley, A.L. (1937) *Wages and income in the United Kingdom since 1860*, Cambridge: Cambridge University Press.

Bowley, A.L. and Burnett-Hurst, A.R. (1915) *Livelihood and poverty: A study in the economic conditions of working class households in Northampton, Warrington, Stanley and Reading*, London: G. Bell & Sons.

Bowley, A.L. and Hogg, M.H. (1925) *Has poverty diminished?*, London: P.S. King and Son.

Bradbury, B. and Jäntti, M. (1999) *Child poverty across industrialized nations*, Florence: UNICEF International Child Development Centre.

Bradbury, B., Micklewright, J. and Jenkins, S.P. (eds) (2001) *The dynamics of child poverty in industrialised countries*, Cambridge: Cambridge University Press.

Bradshaw, J. (1990) *Child poverty and deprivation in the UK*, London: National Children's Bureau.

Bradshaw, J. (ed) (1993) *Budget standards for the United Kingdom*, Aldershot: Avebury.

Bradshaw, J. (2001) 'Child poverty under Labour', in G. Fimister (ed) *An end in sight? Tackling child poverty in the UK*, London: Child Poverty Action Group, pp 9-27.

Bradshaw, J. and Finch, N. (2002) *A comparison of child benefit packages in 22 countries*, DWP Research Report 174, London: Department for Work and Pensions.

Bradshaw, J. and Lynes, T. (1995) *Benefit uprating policy and living standards*, Social Policy Reports 1, York: Social Policy Research Unit, University of York.

Bradshaw, J. and Millar, J. (1991) *Lone-parent families in the UK*, London: HMSO.

Bradshaw, J., Ditch, J., Holmes, H. and Whiteford, P. (1993) 'A comparative study of child support in fifteen countries', *Journal of European Social Policy*, vol 3, no 4, pp 255-71.

Briggs, A. (1961) *Social thought and social action: A study of the work of Seebhom Rowntree 1871-1954*, London: Longman.

Brown, G. (1999) *Chancellor of the Exchequer's budget statement*, 9 March, London: HM Treasury (http://archive.treasury.gov.uk/budget/1999/speech.html, accessed 30 March 2004).

Brown, G. (2000) 'Our children are our future', *Speech by the Chancellor of the Exchequer to the Child Poverty Action Group conference*, London: 15 May.

Burnett, J. (1994) *Idle hands: The experience of unemployment, 1790-1990*, London: Routledge.

Cadbury, E., Matheson, M.C. and Shann, G. (1908) *Women's work and wages* (2nd edn), London: Fisher Unwin.

Callan, T., Nolan, B. and Whelan, C.T. (1993) 'Resources, deprivation and the measurement of poverty', *Journal of Social Policy*, vol 22, no 2, pp 141-72.

Caradog Jones, D. (1934) *The social survey of Merseyside*, London: Hodder and Stoughton.

Carr-Saunders, A.M., Caradog Jones, D. and Moser, C.A. (1958) *A survey of social conditions in England and Wales as illustrated by statistics*, Oxford: Clarendon Press.

Chadwick, E. (1965) *Report on the sanitary condition of the labouring population of Great Britain, 1842*, edited by M.W. Flinn, Edinburgh: Edinburgh University Press.

Coates, K. and Silburn, R. (1970) *Poverty: The forgotten Englishmen*, Harmonsdworth: Penguin.

Coleman, D. (2000) 'Population and family', in A.H. Halsey and J. Webb (eds) *Twentieth century British social trends*, Basingstoke: Macmillan, pp 27-93.

Craig, P. (1991) 'Costs and benefits: a review of research on take-up of income related benefits', *Journal of Social Policy* vol 20, no 4, pp 537-65.

Cross, S. and Golding, P. (1999) 'A poor press? Media reception of the Beveridge lecture', in R. Walker (ed) *Ending child poverty: Popular welfare for the 21st century?*, Bristol: The Policy Press, pp 121-38.

Cunningham, H. (1990) 'The employment and unemployment of children in England c.1680-1851', *Past and Present*, vol 126, pp 115-49.

Cunningham, H. (1995) *Children and childhood in Western society since 1500*, London: Longman.

Daniel, P. and Ivatts, J. (1998) *Children and social policy*, Basingstoke: Macmillan.

Darwin, C. (1998 [1859]) *The origin of species*, Ware: Wordsworth Classics.

Davey Smith, G., Dorling, D. and Shaw, M. (2001) *Poverty, inequality and health in Britain, 1800-2000: A reader*, Bristol: The Policy Press.

Davidoff, L., Doolittle, M., Fink, J. and Holden, K. (1999) *The family story: Blood, contract and intimacy, 1830-1960*, London: Longman.

Davin, L.A. (1996) *Growing up poor: Home, school and street in London, 1870-1914*, London: Rivers Oram Press.

Deacon, A. (1999) 'Rights and responsibilities', in R. Walker (ed) *Ending child poverty: Popular welfare for the 21st century?*, Bristol: The Policy Press, pp 75-82.

Deacon, A. (2002) 'Echoes of Sir Keith? New Labour and the cycle of disadvantage', *Benefits*, vol 10, no 3, pp 179-84.

Deacon, A. and Bradshaw, J. (1983) *Reserved for the poor: The means test in British social policy*, Oxford: Basil Blackwell/Martin Robertson.

DfEE (Department for Education and Employment) (2000) *Departmental report*, London: DfEE.

DoH (Department of Health) (1999) *UN Convention on the Rights of the Child: Second report to the UN committee on the rights of the child by the United Kingdom 1999*, London: The Stationery Office.

Dorsett, R and Heady, C. (1991) 'The take-up of means-tested benefits by working families with children', *Fiscal Studies*, vol 12, no 4, pp 22-32.

DSS (Department of Social Security) (1999) *A new contract for welfare: Children's rights and parents' responsibilities*, White Paper, Cm 4349, London: DSS.

DWP (Department for Work and Pensions) (2003a) *Measuring child poverty consultation: Preliminary conclusions*, London: DWP.

DWP (2003b) *United Kingdom national action plan on social inclusion 2003-05*, London: DWP.

Elias, N. (1994) *The civilising process: The history of manners and state formation and civilisation*, Oxford: Blackwell.

Engels, F. (1969 [1845]) *The condition of the working class in England*, London: Panther.

Falkingham, F. (1986) *Take-up of benefits: A literature review*, Nottingham: Nottingham University.

Field, F. (1985) *What price a child? A historical review of the relative cost of dependants*, London: Policy Studies Institute.

Fimister, G. (2001) 'Introduction', in G. Fimister (ed) *An end in sight? Tackling child poverty in the UK*, London: Child Poverty Action Group, pp 1-8.

Findlay, J. and Wright, R.E. (1996) 'Gender, poverty and the intra-household distribution of resources', *Review of Income and Wealth*, vol 42, no 3, pp 335-51.

Ford, R. and Millar, J. (eds) (1998) *Private lives and public costs: Lone parents and the state*, London: Policy Studies Institute.

Fraser, D. (1976) *The New Poor Law in the nineteenth century*, London: Macmillan.

Fraser, D. (1984) *The evolution of the British welfare state*, Basingstoke: Macmillan.

Fry, V. and Stark, G. (1993) *The take-up of means-tested benefits 1984-90*, London: Institute for Fiscal Studies.

Galton, F. (1998 [1869]) *Hereditary genius* (1869), Bristol: Thoemmes Press.

Gauthier, A.H. (1996) *The state and the family: A comparative analysis of family policies in industrialized countries*, Oxford: Clarendon Press.

George, R.F. (1937) 'A new calculation of the poverty line', *Journal of the Royal Statistical Society*, vol 100, no 1, pp 74-95.

Gillie, A. (2000) 'Rowntree, poverty lines and school boards', in J. Bradshaw and R. Sainsbury (eds) *Getting the measure of poverty: The early legacy of Seebohm Rowntree*, Aldershot: Ashgate, pp 85-108.

Glass, D.V. (ed) (1963) *Social mobility in Britain*, London: Routledge and Kegan Paul.

Glendinning, C. and Millar, J. (1992) '"It all really starts in the family": gender divisions and poverty', in C. Glendinning and J. Millar (eds) *Women and poverty in Britain: The 1990s*, Hemel Hempstead: Harvester Wheatsheaf, pp 3-10.

Glennerster, H. (1995) *British social policy since 1945*, Oxford: Blackwell.

GMB/MPO (Managerial and Professional Officers Union) (1999) *UK school children at work*, London: GMB.

Good, J., Lister, R. and Callender, C. (1998) *Purse or wallet? Gender inequalities and income distribution within families on benefits*, London: Policy Studies Institute.

Goodman, A., Johnson, P. and Webb, S. (1997) *Inequality in the UK*, Oxford: Oxford University Press.

Gordon, D. and Pantazis, C. (1997) *Breadline Britain in the 1990s*, Aldershot: Ashgate.

Gordon, D., Adelman, L., Ashworth, K., Bradshaw, J., Levitas, R., Middleton, S., Pantazis, C., Patsios, D., Payne, S., Townsend, P. and Williams, J. (2000) *Poverty and social exclusion in Britain*, York: Joseph Rowntree Foundation.

Green, A. (1990) *Education and state formation: The rise of education systems in England, France and the USA*, Basingstoke: Macmillan.

Gregg, P., Harkness, S. and Machin, S. (1999) *Child development and family incomes*, York: Joseph Rowntree Foundation.

Hair, P.E.H. (1982) 'Children in society 1850-1950', in T. Barker and M. Drake (eds) *Population and society in Britain 1850-1980*, London: Batsford, pp 34-61.

Harris, J. (1997) *William Beveridge: A biography* (2nd edn), Oxford: Clarendon Press.

Hay, J.R. (1978) *The development of the British welfare state 1880-1975*, London: Edward Arnold.

Hendrick, H. (1994) *Child welfare: England 1872-1989*, London: Routledge.

Hendrick, H. (1997) *Children, childhood and English society, 1880-1990*, Cambridge: Cambridge University Press.

Hendrick, H. (2003) *Child welfare: Historical dimensions, contemporary debate*, Bristol: The Policy Press.

Hennock, E.P. (1991) 'Concepts of poverty in the British social surveys from Charles Booth to Arthur Bowley', in M. Bulmer, K. Bales and K. Kish Sklar (eds) *The social survey in historical perspective*, Cambridge: Cambridge University Press, pp 189-216.

Heywood, C. (2001) *A history of childhood*, Cambridge: Polity Press.

Hill, M.S. and Jenkins, S.P. (2001) 'Poverty amongst British children: chronic or transitory?', in B. Bradbury, S.P. Jenkins and J. Micklewright (eds) *The dynamics of child poverty in industrialised countries*, Cambridge: Cambridge University Press, pp 174-95.

Hill, P. (1940) *The unemployment services: A report prepared for the Fabian Society*, London: Routledge.

HM Treasury (2004) *Child poverty review*, London: HMSO.

Home Office (1998) *Supporting families: A consultation document*, London: Home Office.

Illich, I. (1971) *Deschooling society*, London: Calder & Boyars.

Illich, I. (1982) *Gender*, New York, NY: Pantheon Books.

Jenkins, S.P. and Rigg, J.A. (2001) *The dynamics of poverty in Britain*, London: DWP.

Jenkins, S.P., Schluter, C. and Wagner, G. (2003) 'The dynamics of child poverty: Britain and Germany compared', *Journal of Comparative Family Studies*, vol 34, no 3, pp 337-53.

Johnson, P. and Webb, S. (1989) *Counting people with low incomes: The impact of recent changes in official statistics*, London: Institute for Fiscal Studies.

Kamerman, S.B., Neuman, M., Waldfogel, J. and Brooks-Gunn, J. (2003) *Social policies, family types and child outcomes in selected OECD countries*, OECD social, employment and migration working papers no.6, Paris: OECD.

Kempson, E. (1996) *Life on a low income*, York: Joseph Rowntree Foundation.

Kempson, E., Bryson, A. and Rowlingson, K. (1994) *Hard times? How poor families make ends meet*, London: Policy Studies Institute.

Kerr, S. (1983) *Making ends meet: An investigation into the non-claiming of supplementary pensions*, London: Bedford Square Press.

Koven, S. and Michel, S. (1989) 'Gender and the origins of the welfare state', *Radical History Review*, vol 43, pp 112-19.

Lavalette, M. and Cunningham, S. (2002) 'The sociology of childhood', in B. Goldson, M. Lavalette and J. McKechnie (eds) *Children, welfare and the state*, London: Sage Publications, pp 9-28.

League of Nations (1924) 'Declaration of the rights of the child', *League of Nations Fifth Assembly*, 26 September 1924.

Levitas, R. (1998) *The inclusive society: Social exclusion and New Labour*, Basingstoke: Macmillan.

Lewis, J. (1980) *The politics of motherhood: Child and maternal welfare in England, 1900-39*, London: Croom Helm.

Lewis, J. (1984) *Women in England 1870-1950: Sexual divisions and social change*, Brighton: Wheatsheaf.

Lewis, J. (2001) 'Family change and lone parents as a social problem', in M. May, R. Page and E. Brunsdon (eds) *Understanding social problems: Issues in social policy*, Oxford: Blackwell, pp 37-54.

Lewis, J., Kiernan, K. and Land, H. (1998) *Lone parents in twentieth century Britain*, Oxford: Oxford University Press.

Lister, R. (1990) *The exclusive society: Citizenship and the poor*, London: Child Poverty Action Group.

Low Pay Commission (2004) *The national minimum wage: Protecting young workers*, London: Low Pay Commission.

Lynes, T. (1962) *National assistance and national prosperity*, Occasional Papers on Social Administration, 5, London: G. Bell & Sons.

McCarthy, M. (1986) *Campaigning for the poor: CPAG and the politics of welfare*, London: Croom Helm.

McCulloch, J.R. (1841) *A dictionary, geographical, statistical and historical, of the various countries, places, and principal natural objects in the world. Illustrated with maps* (two volumes), London: Longman, Orme, Brown, Green, and Longmans.

Mack, J. and Lansley, S. (1985) *Poor Britain*, London: George Allen and Unwin.

McKay, S. and Collard, S. (2004) *Developing deprivation questions for the Family Resources Survey*, DWP Information and Analysis Directorate Research Division, Working Paper 13, London: DWP.

Macnicol, J. (1980) *The movement for family allowances 1918-45: A study in social policy development*, London: Heinemann.

Malthus, T.R. (1992 [1803]) *An essay on the principle of population* (edited by D. Winch), Cambridge: Cambridge University Press.

Mayhew, H. (1861-62) *London labour and the London poor: A cyclopædia of the condition and earnings of those that will work, those that cannot work, and those that will not work*, London: Griffin, Bohn, and Company.

Mayhew, H. (1980 [1849-50]) *The Morning Chronicle survey of labour and the poor: The metropolitan districts*, Firle: Caliban.

M'Gonigle, G.C.M and Kirby, J. (1936) *Poverty and public health*, London: Victor Gollancz.

Micklewright, J. (2003) *Child poverty in English speaking countries*, SSRC Applications and Policy Working Paper A03/05, Southampton: Social Statistics Research Centre, University of Southampton.

Middleton, S., Ashworth, K. and Braithwaite, I. (1997) *Small fortunes: Spending on children, childhood poverty and parental sacrifice*, York: Joseph Rowntree Foundation.

Middleton, S., Ashworth, K. and Walker, R. (1994) *Family fortunes: Pressures on parents and children in the 1990s*, London: Child Poverty Action Group.

Mill, J.S. (1991 [1859]) 'On liberty', in *On liberty and other essays* (edited by J. Gray), Oxford: Oxford University Press, pp 1-128.

Millar, J. (1989) *Poverty and the lone-parent family: The challenge to social policy*, Avebury: Gower.

Mitchell, M. (1985) 'The effects of unemployment on the social condition of women and children in the 1930s', *History Workshop*, vol 19, pp 105-27.

Morris, L. (1984) 'Redundancy and patterns of household finance', *Sociological Review*, vol 32, no 3, pp 492-523.

Morris, L. (1990) *The workings of the household,* Cambridge: Polity Press.

Murray, C. (1996) 'The emerging British underclass', in R. Lister (ed) *Charles Murray and the underclass: The developing debate*, London: IEA Health and Welfare Unit with *The Sunday Times*, pp 23-53.

Nicholls, G. (1898-1904) *A history of the English Poor Law in connection with the legislation and other circumstances affecting the condition of the people. Vol. 3 by T. Mackay*, London: Frank Cass.

Nolan, B. and Whelan, C. (1996) *Resources, deprivation and poverty*, Oxford: Clarendon Press.

Oastler, R. (1984 [1830]) Letter on 'Yorkshire slavery', *Leeds Mercury*, 16 October 1830, in D. Fraser *The evolution of the British welfare state* (2nd edn), Basingstoke: Macmillan, Document 1, pp 254-5.

O'Donnell, C. and White, L. (1998) *Invisible hands: A study of child employment in the North*, London: Low Pay Unit.

Oldfield, N. (1992) *Using budget standards to estimate the cost of children*, York: University of York Family Budget Centre.

Oldfield, N. (1993) 'The cost of a child', in J. Bradshaw (ed) *Budget standards for the United Kingdom*, Aldershot: Avebury, pp 177-95.

Oldfield, N. and Yu, A.C.S. (1993) *The cost of a child: Living standards for the 1990s*, London: Child Poverty Action Group.

Oppenheim, C. and Harker, L. (1996) *Poverty: The facts* (3rd edn), London: Child Poverty Action Group.

Orwell, G. (2001 [1937]) *The road to Wigan pier*, London: Penguin.

Padley, R. and Cole, M. (eds) (1940) *Evacuation survey: A report to the Fabian Society*, London: Routledge.

Parker, H. (1998) *Low cost but acceptable: A minimum income standard for the UK*, Bristol: The Policy Press.

Parr, J. (1980) *Labouring children: British immigrant apprentices to Canada, 1869-1924*, London: Croom Helm.

Pedersen, S. (1989) 'The failure of feminism in the making of the British welfare state', *Radical History Review*, vol 43, pp 86-110.

Pedersen, S. (1993) *Family, dependence and the origins of the welfare state: Britain and France 1914-1945*, Cambridge: Cambridge University Press.

Pedersen, S. (2004) *Eleanor Rathbone and the politics of conscience*, New Haven, CT: Yale University Press.

Pember Reeves, M. (1979 [1913]) *Round about a pound a week*, London: Virago.

PEP (Political and Economic Planning) (1952) *Poverty: Ten years after Beveridge*, London: PEP.

Pettit, B. (ed) (1998) *Children and work in the UK: Reassessing the issues*, London: Child Poverty Action Group.

Piachaud, D. (1979) *The cost of a child*, London: Child Poverty Action Group.

Piachaud, D. (1981) 'Peter Townsend and the Holy Grail', *New Society*, vol 57, pp 419-21.

Piachaud, D. (1987) 'Problems in the definition and measurement of poverty', *Journal of Social Policy*, vol 16, no 2, pp 147-64.

Piachaud, D. and Sutherland, H. (2001) 'Child poverty in Britain and the New Labour government', *Journal of Social Policy*, vol 30, no 1, pp 95-118.

Pierson, P. (1994) *Dismantling the welfare state? Reagan, Thatcher and the politics of retrenchment*, Cambridge: Cambridge University Press.

Pilgrim Trust (1938) *Men without work: A report made to the Pilgrim Trust*, Cambridge: Cambridge University Press.

Pinchbeck, I. and Hewitt, M. (1973) *Children in English society*, London: Routledge and Kegan Paul.

Pollock, L.A. (1983) *Forgotten children: Parent child relations from 1500 to 1900*, Cambridge: Cambridge University Press.

Poovey, M. (1998) *A history of the modern fact: Problems of knowledge in the sciences of wealth and society*, Chicago, IL: University of Chicago Press.

Rathbone, E.F. (1924) *The disinherited family: A plea for direct provision for the costs of child maintenance through family allowances*, London: Edward Arnold.

Rathbone, E. (1927) *The ethics and economics of family endowment*, London: Epworth.

Report of the departmental committee on sickness benefit claims under the National Insurance Act, 1914, in P. Thane (1996) *Foundations of the welfare state* (2nd edn) London: Longman, Document 8, pp 315-17.

Ridge, T. (2002) *Child poverty and social exclusion: From a child's perspective*, Bristol: The Policy Press.

Ringen, S. (1988) 'Direct and indirect measures of poverty', *Journal of Social Policy*, vol 17, no 3, pp 351-65.

Rose, M.E. (1966) 'The allowance system under the New Poor Law', *The Economic History Review*, vol 3, pp 607-20.

Rose, M.E. (1972) *The relief of poverty, 1834-1914*, London: Macmillan.

Rowlingson, K. and McKay, S. (1998) *The growth of lone parenthood: Diversity and dynamics*, London: Policy Studies Institute.

Rowlingson, K. and McKay, S. (2001) *Lone parent families: Gender, class and state*, London: Pearson Education.

Rowntree, B.S. (1902) *Poverty: A study of town life* (2nd edn), London: Macmillan.

Rowntree, B.S. (1918) *The human needs of labour*, London: Thomas Nelson and Sons.

Rowntree, B.S. (1937) *The human needs of labour*, London: Longmans, Green and Co.

Rowntree, B.S. (1942) *Poverty and progress: A second social survey of York*, London: Longmans, Green and Co.

Rowntree, B.S. and Lavers, G.R. (1951) *Poverty and the welfare state: A third social survey of York dealing only with economic questions*, London: Longmans, Green and Co.

Rowntree, B.S. and Sherwell, A. (1899) *The temperance problem and social reform* (4th edn), London: Hodder and Stoughton.

Royal Commission on the Poor Laws (1833) *Extracts from the information received by His Majesty's Commissioners, as to the administration and operation of the Poor-Laws*, Published by Authority, London: B. Fellowes.

Royal Commission on the Poor Laws (1909) *Report of the Royal Commission on the Poor Laws and relief of distress* (the Majority Report), London: His Majesty's Stationery Office.

Ruskin, J. (1994 [1867]) *Time and tide by Weare and Tyne: Twenty-five letters to a working man of Sunderland on the laws of work*, London: Routledge/Thoemmes.

Ruxton, S. and Bennett, F. (2001) *Including children? Developing a coherent approach to child poverty and social exclusion across Europe*, Brussels: Euronet.

Save the Children Fund (1933) *Unemployment and the child: An enquiry*, London: Save the Children Fund.

Sen, A. (1983) 'Poor, relatively speaking', *Oxford Economic Papers*, vol 35, no 2, pp 153-69.

Sen, A. (1985) 'A sociological approach to the measurement of poverty: a reply to Professor Peter Townsend', *Oxford Economic Papers*, vol 37, no 4, pp 669-76.

Sen, A. (1987) *The standard of living: The Tanner lectures, Clare Hall, 1985* (edited by G. Hawthorn), Cambridge: Cambridge University Press.

Skocpol, T. (1992) *Protecting soldiers and mothers: The political origins of social policy in the United States*, Cambridge, MA: Harvard University Press.

Smiles, S. (1885) *Thrift*, London: John Murray.

Smiles, S. (1897) *Self-help* (revised edn), London: John Murray.

Smith, A. (1976 [1776]) *An inquiry into the nature and causes of the wealth of nations* (edited by E. Cannan), Chicago, IL: University of Chicago Press.

Smith, G. (2000) 'Schools', in A.H. Halsey and J. Webb (eds) *Twentieth century British social trends*, Basingstoke: Macmillan.

Smith, T. and Noble, M. (1995) *Education divides: Poverty and schooling in the 1990s*, London: Child Poverty Action Group.

Spring Rice, M.G. (1981 [1939]) *Working-class wives: Their health and conditions* (2nd edn), London: Virago.

Stigler, S.M. (1999) *Statistics on the table: The history of statistical concepts and methods*, Cambridge, MA: Harvard University Press.

Stone, L. (1977) *The family, sex and marriage in England 1500-1800*, London: Weidenfeld and Nicholson.

Sutherland, H. and Piachaud, D. (2001) 'Reducing child poverty in Britain: an assessment of government policy, 1997-2001', *Economic Journal*, vol 111, no 469, pp 85-101.

Sutherland, H., Sefton, T. and Piachaud, D. (2003) *Poverty in Britain: The impact of government policy since 1997*, York: Joseph Rowntree Foundation.

Szreter, S. (1996) *Fertility, class and gender in Britain, 1860-1940*, Cambridge: Cambridge University Press.

Tawney, R.H. (1922) *Secondary education for all*, London: The Labour Party.

Tawney, R.H. (1938 [1926]) *Religion and the rise of capitalism*, Harmondsworth: Penguin.

Thane, P. (1996) *Foundations of the welfare state* (2nd edition), London: Longman.

Thompson, E.P. and Yeo, E. (1971) *The unknown Mayhew*, London: Merlin Press.

Titmuss, R. (1943) *Birth, poverty and wealth: A study of infant mortality*, London: Hamish Hamilton.

Titmuss, R. (1958) *Essays on the welfare state*, London: Allen and Unwin.

Titmuss, R. (1962) *Income distribution and social change*, London: Allen and Unwin.

Titmuss, R. and Titmuss, K. (1942) *Parents revolt: A study of the declining birth-rate in acquisitive societies*, London: Secker and Warburg.

Tout, H. (1938) *The standard of living in Bristol*, Bristol: Arrowsmith.

Townsend, P. (1957) *The family life of old people*, London: Routledge & Kegan Paul.

Townsend, P. (1962) 'The meaning of poverty', *British Journal of Sociology*, vol 13, no 3, pp 210-27.

Townsend, P. (1979) *Poverty in the United Kingdom*, London: Penguin.

Townsend, P. (1985) 'A sociological approach to the measurement of poverty – a rejoinder to Professor Amartya Sen', *Oxford Economic Papers*, vol 37, no 4, pp 659-68.

Townsend, P. and Davidson, N. (1982) *Inequalities in health: The Black Report*, Harmondsworth: Penguin.

TUC (Trades Union Congress) (1997) *Working classes: A TUC report on school age labour in England*, London: TUC.

UN (United Nations) (1996) *Convention on the Rights of the Child*, London: The Stationery Office.

UNICEF (2000) *A league table of child poverty in rich nations*, Innocenti Report Card No. 1, June 2000, Florence: UNICEF Innocenti Research Centre.

Veit-Wilson, J. (1986a) 'Paradigms of poverty: a rehabilitation of B.S. Rowntree', *Journal of Social Policy*, vol 15, no 1, pp 69-99.

Veit-Wilson, J. (1986b) 'Paradigms of poverty: a reply to Peter Townsend and Hugh McLachlan', *Journal of Social Policy*, vol 15, no 4, pp 503-07.

Veit-Wilson, J. (1987) 'Consensual approaches to poverty lines and social security', *Journal of Social Policy*, vol 16, no 2, pp 183-211.

Veit-Wilson, J. (1992) 'Muddle or mendacity? The Beveridge Committee and the poverty line', *Journal of Social Policy*, vol 21, no 3, pp 269-301.

Veit-Wilson, J. (1994) 'Condemned to deprivation? Beveridge's responsibility for the invisibility of poverty', in J. Hills, J. Ditch, and H. Glennerster (eds) *Beveridge and social security*, Oxford: Clarendon Press, pp 97-117.

Vickerstaff, S. (2003) 'Education and training', in J. Baldock, N. Manning and S. Vickerstaff (eds) *Social policy* (2nd edn), Oxford: Oxford University Press, pp 362-86.

Vincent, D. (1991) *Poor citizens: The state and the poor in twentieth century Britain*, London: Longman.

Vleminckx, K. and Smeeding, T. (2001) *Child well-being, child poverty and child policy in modern nations: What do we know?*, Bristol: The Policy Press.

Wakefield, H.R., Chandler, F., Lansbury, G. and Webb, Mrs S. (1909) *Separate report [on the Poor Laws and relief of distress]* (the Minority Report of the Royal Commission on the Poor Laws), London: His Majesty's Stationery Office.

Walker, R. (1987) 'Consensual approaches to the definition of poverty: towards an alternative methodology', *Journal of Social Policy*, vol 16, no 2, pp 213-26.

Walker, R. (1999a) 'Introduction', in R. Walker (ed) *Ending child poverty: Popular welfare for the 21st century*, Bristol: The Policy Press, pp 3-5.

Walker, R. (1999b) 'Dimensions of the debate: reflections on the Beveridge Lecture', in R. Walker (ed) *Ending child poverty: Popular welfare for the 21st century*, Bristol: The Policy Press, pp 139-57.

Walker, R. with Ashworth, K. (1994) *Poverty dynamics: Issues and examples*, Aldershot: Avebury.

Ward, H. (2000) 'Poverty and family cohesion', in J. Bradshaw and R. Sainsbury (eds) *Getting the measure of poverty: The early legacy of Seebohm Rowntree*, Aldershot: Ashgate, pp 207-23.

Weber, M. (1976) *The Protestant ethic and the spirit of capitalism* (translated by T. Parsons) (2nd edn), London: Allen and Unwin.

Webster, C. (1982) 'Healthy or hungry thirties?', *History Workshop*, vol 13, pp 110-29.

Webster, C. (1985) 'Health, welfare and unemployment during the depression', *Past and Present*, vol 109, pp 204-30.

Wedderburn, D.C. (1962) 'Poverty in Britain today: the evidence', *Sociological Review*, vol 10, no 3, pp 257-82.

Welshman, J. (2002) 'The cycle of deprivation and the concept of the underclass', *Benefits*, vol 10, no 3, pp 199-205.

Whelan, C., Layte, R., Maître, B. and Nolan, B. (2001) 'Income, deprivation and economic strain: an analysis of the European Community Household Panel', *European Sociological Review*, vol 17, no 4, pp 357-72.

White, F.W. (2001 [1928]) 'Natural and social selection: a 'Blue-Book' analysis', in G. Davey Smith. D. Dorling and M. Shaw (eds) *Poverty, inequality and health in Britain 1800-2000: A reader*, Bristol: The Policy Press, pp 162-72.

Whitehead, M. (1987) *The health divide: Inequalities in health in the 1980s*, London: Health Education Council.

Williams, K. (1981) *From pauperism to poverty*, London: Routledge and Kegan Paul.

Wilson, E. (1977) *Women and the welfare state*, London: Tavistock.

Wollstonecraft, M. (1992 [1792]) *A vindication of the rights of woman*, edited by M. Brody, Harmondsworth: Penguin.

Woods, R.I. (1996) 'The population of Britain in the nineteenth century', in M. Anderson (ed) *British population history: From the Black Death to the present day*, Cambridge: Cambridge University Press, pp 281-357.

WPSC (Work and Pensions Select Committee) (2004) *Child poverty in the UK* (The Second Report of Session 2003-2004), London: House of Commons.

Young, M. and Willmott, P. (1986) *Family and kinship in East London* (reprinted with a new introduction), London: Routledge and Kegan Paul.

Yu, A.C.S. (1993) 'The low cost budget', in J. Bradshaw (ed) *Budget standards for the United Kingdom*, Aldershot: Avebury, pp 196-215.

Zelizer, V.A. (1985) *Pricing the priceless child: The changing social value of children*, Princeton, NJ: Princeton University Press.

Index

Page numbers in *italics* refer to tables or figures.

Webster, C. 66
Wedderburn, Dorothy 23-4, 97
White, Frank F. 19
widows 90
Williams, K. 18, 49
Willmott, Peter 22
Wollstoncroft, Mary 48-9
women
  and education 48-9
  mother and baby support measures
    69-71
  protection versus dependency 38-9, 42
  relationship to child welfare 26, 50-1,
    63-4, 77-8
  self-deprivation 77-8
  wage differentials 63, 71-2, 82, 84
Women's Co-operative Guild 69
Women's Health Enquiry Committee
  77-8
Women's work and wages (Cadbury et al,
  1908) 63
work conditions
  early empirical studies 16-18
  use of sentiment and anecdote 22, 36-8
Worker's Tax Credit 95-6
workhouses *15*, 56-7, 61
  and education 46-7
Working Families Tax Credit 95-6
working mothers 101-2

Y

Young, Michael 22
Yu, A.C.S. 103

Z

Zelizer, V.A. 118

Other titles in the Studies in Poverty, Inequality and Social Exclusion series

Childhood poverty and social exclusion
From a child's perspective
Tess Ridge

"The sharp observations of these young citizens on their schooling, on problems in their neighbourhood and on the deficiencies of their leisure opportunities, set an agenda for any practitioner who aspires to tackle family poverty." *Community Care*

"... a vivid and comprehensive picture of what it is like to grow up poor in Britain today." *Journal of Social policy*

Without a deeper understanding of poverty as a lived experience in childhood, policies targeted at eradicating child poverty may fail. Using child-centred research methods to explore children's own accounts of their lives, this original book presents a rare and valuable opportunity to understand the issues and concerns that low-income children themselves identify as important. The findings raise critical issues for both policy and practice.

Paperback £18.99 US$29.95 ISBN 1 86134 362 0
234 x 156mm 192 pages October 2002

Child poverty in the developing world
David Gordon, Shailen Nandy, Christina Pantazis, Simon Pemberton and Peter Townsend

This report provides a summary of the results from a major international research project, funded by UNICEF, on child rights and child poverty in the developing world. It presents the first ever scientific measurement of the extent and depth of child poverty in developing regions. This measurement is based upon internationally agreed definitions arising from the international framework of child rights.

Paperback £9.99 US$15.00 ISBN 1 86134 559 3
A4 Report (297 x 210mm) 44 pages October 2003

Patterns of poverty across Europe
Richard Berthoud

Using new EU-wide data, this report shows very different patterns of poverty across Europe, depending on the benchmark used. The findings have important implications for the spatial distribution of poverty within and between countries (including the UK) and for the development of anti-poverty policy across the EU.

Paperback £12.99 US$20.95 ISBN 1 86134 574 7
A4 Report (297 x 210mm) 60 pages March 2004

Breadline Europe
The measurement of poverty
Edited by David Gordon and Peter Townsend

"... an undeniable contribution to understanding the complexity of poverty, its measurement and relations with inequality and social exclusion ... will be useful for researchers and valuable for students interested in poverty issues." *The British Journal of Social Work*

"The Policy Press is fast carving out a niche for itself in producing up-to-date and accessible material on issues directly and indirectly relevant to policy. This book is exemplary on these counts." *Sociology*

"... one of the most authoritative works on poverty." *European Journal of Social Security*

The first book to examine poverty in Europe within the international framework agreed at the 1995 World Summit on Social Development, *Breadline Europe* provides a scientific and international basis for the analysis and reduction of poverty. With contributions from leading European poverty experts, it presents up-to-date and cutting-edge international poverty research in one volume.

Paperback £19.99 US$29.95 ISBN 1 86134 292 6
234 x 156mm 480 pages December 2000

World poverty
New policies to defeat an old enemy
Edited by Peter Townsend and David Gordon

"The great value of this collection is that it tackles the complexities of international poverty analysis head on. The authors leave us with the inspiration to pursue a clear and ambitious research agenda and the campaigners amongst us may well be spurred on by the Manifesto for International Action to Defeat Poverty laid out in the Appendix. *World poverty* is essential reading for social policy students and scholars."
SPA News

World poverty is an indispensable book offering fresh insights into how to tackle poverty worldwide. With contributions from leading scholars in the field both internationally and in the UK, the book asks whether existing international and national policies are likely to succeed in reducing poverty across the world. It concludes that they are not and that a radically different international strategy is needed.

Paperback £25.00 US$35.00 ISBN 1 86134 395 7
Hardback £55.00 US$69.95 ISBN 1 86134 396 5
234 x 156mm 480 pages September 2002

Also available

Child well-being, child poverty and child policy in modern nations
What do we know?
Edited by Koen Vleminckx and Timothy M. Smeeding

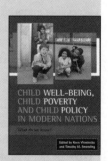

"... the breadth and scope of this collection is astonishing."
Local Government Studies

The revised edition of this best-selling book includes a new Foreword by Professor Gøsta Esping-Andersen and an updated introduction and conclusion providing insights into the key issues. The book's contributors are all leading experts in economics, sociology and social policy who have studied the extent of child poverty, its consequences for children and the effectiveness of policies of prevention.

Paperback £25.00 US$35.00 ISBN 1 86134 253 5
Hardback £50.00 US$69.95 ISBN 1 86134 254 3
216 x 148mm 592 pages February 2001

Child welfare
Historical dimensions, contemporary debate
Harry Hendrick

"Hendrick has provided us with a book to be appreciated and savoured, one offering students and the general reader a shrewd and intelligent overview of child welfare policy. Here is a standard text, one unlikely to be bettered for a long time." *Youth & Policy*

"... an engrossing book in which one is constantly forced to reflect on connections between historical developments and current shifts in children's services." *SPA News*

This book offers a provocative account of contemporary policies on child welfare and the ideological thrust behind them and provides an informed historical perspective on the evolution of child welfare during the last century.

Paperback £18.99 US$29.95 ISBN 1 86134 477 5
Hardback £55.00 US$59.95 ISBN 1 86134 478 3
234 x 156mm 304 pages February 2003

Children, family and the state
Decision-making and child participation
Nigel Thomas

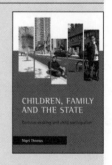

"... a stimulating, readable and accessible book." *Child and Family Social Work*

"... belongs on the reading list of any qualifying or post-qualifying professional course which aims to address the present rather than the past." *Community Care*

"... essential reading for professionals who work with children in care settings." *Family Matters*

Children, family and the state examines different theories of childhood, children's rights and the relationship between children, parents and the state. Focusing on children who are looked after by the state, it reviews the changing objectives of the care system and the extent to which children have been involved in decisions about their care.

Paperback £18.99 US$29.95 ISBN 1 86134 448 1
234 x 156mm 256 pages October 2002

Ordering details overleaf

To order further copies of this publication or any other Policy Press titles please contact:

In the UK and Europe:
Marston Book Services, PO Box 269, Abingdon,
Oxon, OX14 4YN, UK
Tel: +44 (0)1235 465500
Fax: +44 (0)1235 465556
Email: direct.orders@marston.co.uk

In the USA and Canada:
ISBS, 920 NE 58th Street, Suite 300, Portland, OR
97213-3786, USA
Tel: +1 800 944 6190 (toll free)
Fax: +1 503 280 8832
Email: info@isbs.com

In Australia and New Zealand:
DA Information Services, 648 Whitehorse Road
Mitcham, Victoria 3132, Australia
Tel: +61 (3) 9210 7777
Fax: +61 (3) 9210 7788
E-mail: service@dadirect.com.au

Further information about all of our titles can be
found on our website:

www.policypress.org.uk